START & RUN AN
ESL TEACHING BUSINESS

START & RUN AN
ESL TEACHING BUSINESS

T. Nicole Pankratz

Self-Counsel Press
(a division of)
International Self-Counsel Press Ltd.
USA   Canada

Self-Counsel Press acknowledges the financial support of the Government of Canada through the Book Publishing Industry Development Program (BPIDP) for our publishing activities.

Printed in Canada.

First edition: 2006

Library and Archives Canada Cataloguing in Publication

Pankratz, Nicole, 1969–

    Start and run an ESL teaching business / T. Nicole Pankratz. — 1st ed.

(Self-counsel business series)
Accompanied by a CD-ROM.
ISBN-13: 978-1-55180-649-5
ISBN-10: 1-55180-649-5

1. English language—Study and teaching as a second language. 2. Language schools. 3. Tutors and tutoring. 4. New business enterprises. I. Title. II. Series.
PE1128.A2P36 2006   420'.7   C2006-901134-6

Self-Counsel Press
(a division of)
International Self-Counsel Press Ltd.

1704 North State Street	1481 Charlotte Road
Bellingham, WA 98225	North Vancouver, BC V7J 1H1
USA	Canada

For Jade and Panda

CONTENTS

CHECKLISTS

SAMPLES

NOTICE TO READERS

ACKNOWLEDGMENTS

I would like to thank several people for helping me bring this book to life. First, thank you to Richard Day of Self-Counsel Press for accepting my book proposal in the first place, and for welcoming me aboard the SCP team. I would also like to thank senior editor Barbara Kuhne for her support and encouragement, and for assigning me such a thoughtful and experienced editor, Sharon Boglari.

Next, I would like to thank all of the talented administrators, teachers, and support staff I have had the pleasure of working alongside over the past decade or so. Thanks also to the hundreds of students I have met in classrooms and coffee shops, for sharing your opinions and teaching me so much about what works and what does not.

Lastly, thank you Jade and Panda (aka Derek) for your patience and understanding, and for allowing me to disappear into my lair for interminable hours until the book was at last complete.

INTRODUCTION

The information in this book is based on my decade of experience working in the English as a Second Language (ESL) industry.

Over the years, I have worn many hats — teacher, tutor, program coordinator, textbook writer, curriculum developer, and teacher trainer. I have worked in large cities and small towns, and in a variety of institutions, large and small, well established and just barely up and running. I have worked with students of all ages from more than 40 countries; students with visual impairment, hearing loss, or physical challenges; and students with unforgettable stories of both hardship and hope. I have worked solo and with teams of professionals, some effective and others less so.

During this time, I have learned that the ESL industry is ideal for people with an entrepreneurial spirit. Although it is related to education, ESL is more about "business" than "school." Those who do well in the ESL industry understand that in many ways, students are customers who buy products and services — in most cases, English lessons and homestay accommodation — and have certain expectations about their purchases.

Like customers in a store or restaurant, ESL students will complain about products and services they consider unsatisfactory or that are not meeting their expectations. And with a multitude of schools and tutorial services to choose from, dissatisfied students will take their money and their language-acquisition goals elsewhere. For this reason, it is wise for ESL business owners to keep their personal philosophy of education in check — however interesting and profound — and instead focus on getting to know the needs, desires, and perceptions of the students they aim to teach.

Sometimes new business owners with an education or teaching background have trouble understanding their role in the private ESL industry. For example, they may feel it is their obligation to teach international students Western values, or even about life in general. While their intentions may be noble, they often fail to see the big picture or reality of the situation. International students do not come to North America to become Westernized. They may want to learn about Western culture and beliefs, but more often than not, they want to learn English so that they will be able to communicate better with other people about their own culture or belief system. Or they may simply want to prepare for tests that will ultimately lead to a better job, entrance into university, or higher status in their home country.

This book is not for people who have grand ideas about "educating" international students or immigrants. Rather, it is for people who are interested in providing students with the products and services they need, ask for, and are prepared to pay for. It is especially suited to people with some teaching experience and a sincere interest in working with people from other countries.

HOW THE BOOK IS ORGANIZED

This book is divided into four parts. Part 1 contains an overview of the ESL industry in North America. It also provides you with general information on typical ESL schools, tutorial services, and related businesses. The suitability test at the end of the section will help you identify the kind of ESL venture that best suits you.

Part 2 covers the ins and outs of starting an ESL tutorial service. It contains detailed descriptions of what you need to think about and have in place before you start your service, and provides examples from real businesses. At the end of Part 2 are exercises to help you make decisions about your business — your target group of students, the kinds of programs you will offer, where you will run your service. The decisions you make and the information you record in these exercises can become part of your business plan.

Part 3 is devoted solely to information about ESL schools. At the end of this section are exercises that will help you answer key questions necessary for the development of your business plan.

In Part 4, you will start to develop your business plan. This section covers practical topics such as where to find financing, how to name your business, what legal structures to consider, and what you need to get your ESL business off the ground.

HOW TO USE THIS BOOK

The best way to use this book is to first read through it entirely and get a feel for the ESL industry and what is involved in starting a tutoring business or a school. Then by revisiting Part 1, you can think about what role you want to play in the industry and decide which type of business best suits your interests and aptitudes. Refer back to either Part 2 (Starting and Running an ESL Tutorial Service) or Part 3

(Starting and Running an ESL School) and get started on some of the exercises that will become part of your business plan. The exercises are included on the CD-ROM in MS Word and PDF formats, so you can adapt them to suit your particular situation. For easy reference, the samples from the book are also on the CD; you can refer to the samples when you are doing the exercises.

Taking a second look at Part 4, you can begin to identify some of the things you need to know, find out, and do to make your business legal. Use the exercises at the end of Part 4 to get started.

Once you have read the book and worked through the exercises, you will be well prepared for the next step — opening the doors of your new business! And chances are, you will be a welcome addition to this exciting industry that promises both financial gain and the opportunity to put to use your creative energy, management skills, and entrepreneurial spirit. Good luck!

Part 1

ESL INDUSTRY OVERVIEW

Chapter 1

ESL FACTS AND FIGURES

Since the early 1980s, North America's English as a Second Language (ESL) industry has grown by leaps and bounds, and now generates around US$14 billion a year in tuition fees, accommodation, and other related services.

According to an article on the ESL industry in the *Province* (Vancouver) on October 3, 2004, many international students would prefer to study English in the United States because of its economic strength and the easy-to-understand accents of its citizens. Canada, however, is the less expensive choice of the two and is easier to access with regard to visas.

While the future of ESL-related businesses in North America is promising, it is important to understand that the ESL industry is somewhat fickle, as it is tied to the global economy and tourism. The Asian economic crisis in the late 1990s, for example, resulted in a sharp decline in the number of Asian international students coming to North America. Then there was September 11, 2001, and the outbreak of Severe Acute Respiratory Syndrome (SARS), followed by Bovine Spongiform Encephalopathy (BSE, or mad cow disease), all of which affected the number of students coming to the United States and Canada.

The ESL industry is also subject to a great deal of change with regard to visa laws. Business owners need to keep themselves aware of new rules and information, since changes can increase or decrease the number of international students and immigrants allowed to enter North America.

Industry associations are another important influence on the ESL industry. Decisions made by industry associations can affect a school's hiring practices and ability to market effectively. One of the roles of an association is to establish a clear set of ethical and professional standards for schools to follow. The American Association of Intensive English Programs, for example, requires its member schools to hire instructors with a minimum of a master's degree in Teaching English as a Second Language (TESL) or a related field, or experience appropriate to their course assignments. Reaping the marketing benefits of belonging to an organization such as this means following their hiring rules, even if you do not subscribe to the logic of those rules. Opting out of association membership means making your own standards, but it also means you may lose credibility in the eyes of students, agents, and government officials who decide which schools are permitted to generate student visa forms and documents.

Whichever choice you make, it is important to stay aware of trends in industry regulations and how the regulations may affect your business.

Finally, there are other trends to keep in mind. The reasons for students choosing to venture overseas differ from country to country, and sometimes even within the same country. It is important to know the goals of the students you wish to reach, and understand that a future batch of students of the same age and from the same country might be looking for a slightly different type of program.

In short, to start and maintain an ESL business in North America, new and experienced business owners alike need to keep abreast of global issues and shifts in people's reasons for acquiring a second language. They also need to monitor and understand the students themselves. That is, they need to know how many students are out there, where they are from, where they are studying and why they chose to study there, what they are hoping to gain from their overseas experiences, and why they are trying to master English in the first place.

To give you an idea of what your research might uncover, here is a snapshot of the North American ESL market at the time this book was written.

INTERNATIONAL STUDENTS

According to a report on international students published by the Institute of International Education, the United States welcomed more than 565,000 international students in the 2004/2005 school year. (Thousands more entered the country with visitor visas, and many attended English classes at private language institutions.) India is the leading country of origin, followed by China, South Korea, and Japan. These four countries combined contribute 40 percent of the international-student population in the United States. Other countries include Taiwan, Mexico, Turkey, Germany, Thailand, and Indonesia. California continues to host the highest percentage of international students in the United States, followed by New York and Texas.

More than half of the students who come to the United States choose to study at large universities, with business and management being the two most popular fields. However, an increasing number of students are enrolling in pre-academic intensive English programs.

In Canada, the situation is much the same, although on a smaller scale. Approximately 60,000 international students are currently attending universities, private institutes, and colleges in Canada. (In reality, the number is higher, given the great number of short-term students who are attending schools without a visa.)

Almost 70 percent of students settle in two provinces: British Columbia and Ontario. And students from three key nations — South Korea, China, and Japan — make up nearly half the entire number of international students. Other countries of origin include France, India, Mexico, Germany, Taiwan, and Hong Kong.

Regardless of where in North America international students choose to study, their reasons for studying overseas are usually the same:

- To develop their English-speaking skills

- To enhance their academic English performance so they can get higher scores on tests and perhaps gain entrance into a North American college or university

In the end, their goal is to increase their chances of landing a good job in their home country.

IMMIGRANTS

In addition to international students, the ESL industry caters to non-English-speaking immigrants. Some immigrants invest heavily in their children's English education, and many hire private tutors to help their children keep up in public school classes. And some immigrants may hire private tutors for themselves, or seek out conversation classes or speaking clubs for social and educational reasons.

Each year, thousands of adult immigrants in North America attend government-funded ESL programs that are free of charge. These programs are for newcomers who are struggling to pay their rent and bills and do not have money to pay for lessons in basic English.

In the United States, over a million adult learners register in government-sponsored programs every year, representing nearly 40 percent of all adult-education enrollment. And, according to the Center for Adult English Language Acquisition (CAELA), there are long waiting lists for classes. (Find out more about CAELA at www.cal.org/caela.) In 2005, the Office of Vocational and Adult Education agreed there are significant waiting lists, citing three examples:

- At the Queens Library in New York City, two-thirds of the 1,100 people on ESL class waiting lists are not able to get a space in a class in a given year.

- The King County Literacy Coalition in Seattle, Washington, reports that there are 3,000 students on waiting lists for ESL classes. The wait is from six months to a year. At Lake Washington Technical College, the wait for a space in a class is up to six months.

- In San Jose, California, more than 4,000 people were reportedly on waiting lists. (More than 13,500 adults are enrolled in ESL classes in San Jose.)

In Canada, the situation is similar, and has been for some time. According to the National Network for LINC/ELSA/MIIP-ESL Providers, in 2003 there were 766 immigrants on the waiting lists for classes in Calgary. More than 960 others were in line for assessment and referral.

INDUSTRY NEEDS AND TRENDS IN YOUR AREA

Because in many ways the ESL industry hinges on constant change, emerging businesses need to be creative, flexible, and adaptable in order to succeed. The only constant in the ESL world is this: your students are your customers. This means that much of your job as a new business owner will be to understand industry needs and trends in your area.

Finding specific information about the ESL industry in your country and in your area is relatively simple, thanks to the Internet. Every school worth noting has a website, which will provide you with information about your competitors' programs, prices, and staff. The Internet also gives you access to ESL industry associations, which feature links to member schools and other related businesses, as well as useful industry information that may be relevant to your business's future. Business- and immigration-related statistics are also available online.

In-person interviews with people in the industry, and even international students themselves, can also help you get a sense of the market needs in your area. But before doing personal interviews, check out a few ESL chat rooms or weblogs to find out what issues and concerns are on students' minds. Simply doing a search for the term "ESL weblog" on the web, you will find a number of sites where students from all over North America share information on resources and study tips, as well as complaints about common woes — culture shock, loneliness, boredom, and the high cost of living and studying abroad.

Learning as much as you can about what students like, dislike, or find lacking during their overseas stay can help you determine what kind of business is worth investing in, not to mention what features to offer in order to set your business apart from those of your competitors.

Chapter **2**

ESL BUSINESS OPTIONS

The ESL industry is ripe with entrepreneurial potential. Within the industry there are many business options, the two most common of which are starting and running a tutorial service, and starting and running a school. However, as anyone who has dipped his or her toes in the ESL pool knows, there is a lot more to the industry than just tutorial services and schools. Product and service options abound. Indeed, there appears to be something for everyone, provided you carefully watch and listen to market trends, seize opportunities when they arise, and treat your "customers" with care, whether they are students, parents, teachers, or school administrators.

This chapter provides an overview of tutorial services and schools, as well as ideas about alternative business possibilities that you might consider adding to your business in the future to either enhance enrollment or make additional money.

If you are not sure which option best suits you, you can take the suitability test at the end of this chapter.

STARTING A TUTORIAL SERVICE

Tutors play an important role in the ESL industry. They offer students what can be difficult to get in a school environment — one-on-one attention, a chance to focus on specific areas of need or interest, and potential friendship with a native English speaker.

Tutorial services vary in size, formality, and target market. Some operate out of a store-front location, while others are home-based businesses that use a public location such as a coffee shop, library, or food court as the "classroom." Many tutors hold lessons in their own homes. Some even teach in their students' homes or homestays. This is most often the case when it comes to tutoring school-aged children.

Students

For many students, hiring a tutor is a normal part of school life. In Asia, tutoring is common, so students who study abroad often seek extra help in their quest to master the English language. Some even prefer to work exclusively with a tutor instead of attending classes in a school. Adult international students often have budgets that allow for after-school help. And school-aged international students often receive money from their parents to hire a tutor.

Immigrants often hire tutors to help prepare their children for post-secondary education. Some even hire tutors for their own educational and social pursuits.

Programs

Most adult international students hope to find North American friends whom they can confide in and share experiences with. However, it is sometimes difficult for international students to befriend local people. In place of friends and the opportunity for "free English practice," some students opt for a conversation tutor — someone who will patiently listen to them speak, correct their mistakes, and teach them conversation techniques, everyday expressions, and even a bit of slang, in a non-threatening, noncompetitive environment.

Other adult students need a tutor to help them study for rigorous exams, such as the Test of English as a Foreign Language (TOEFL), or review difficult material from their daily classes. Some businesspeople hire tutors to help them with specific skills (e.g., pronunciation) or to help them understand and process North American business practices.

School-aged students attending North American schools need tutors to help them keep up with their English-speaking classmates. Sometimes the tutor's role is to help them with their homework.

Locations and schedules

Tutors and students can meet in a variety of places, including the student's home, the tutor's home, a coffee shop or cafeteria, or a tutorial center. Tutors are usually expected to work flexible hours, including the after-school period, evenings, and weekends.

Tutorial fees

Tutorial fees normally range from US$15 to US$40 an hour, depending on lesson content, and preparation time and travel time required by the tutor, if applicable. Some tutoring organizations also have registration fees.

To explore more detailed information on ESL tutorial services, please see Part 2 of this book.

STARTING A SCHOOL

ESL schools welcome students from around the globe and come in a variety of sizes — some cater to as few as five students, while others serve more than 1,000. Most private ESL schools feature a wide range of conversation-based academic courses, accommodation services, and, in some cases, extracurricular activities.

Students

Most students come to North America to put into practice what they have learned in school in their home country. This is especially true for students who come from countries with a homogeneous population, such as South Korea and Japan, where few foreign-born people live. In such circumstances, being able to speak English gives people a competitive edge in the job market. With little opportunity to practice speaking English in their home country, they head to North America to learn English in an English environment. Most private-institute owners understand that what students want more than anything is the opportunity to speak English inside and outside the classroom. Schools that do not offer student-centered, conversation-based programs do not last long.

Many students come to North America with the intention of attending local colleges and universities. In order to get accepted, however, they must pass the Test of English as a Foreign Language (TOEFL). Developed by the Educational Testing Service (ETS), the TOEFL is used as an academic measurement tool in approximately 200 countries. Preparing for the test is challenging. Most private ESL schools offer TOEFL and other academic-preparation classes as electives.

Many students come to North America to prepare for another important test — the Test of English for International Communication (TOEIC). Also created by ETS, the TOEIC is used to measure a person's potential English ability in the international business world. In many countries, employers require applicants to list their TOEIC scores on their résumé.

Ever-increasing numbers of students are interested in business classes, as well as business internship programs, where students both attend classes and work for North American companies.

Programs and courses

Most ESL schools feature full-time and part-time programs. A typical full-time student will attend 25 to 30 hours of classes a week. A typical part-time student will attend 15 to 18 hours of classes a week.

While many schools offer a wide range of programs — general, academic, business — almost all schools offer classes that help students develop their speaking, listening, reading, and writing skills. Sample 1 shows a typical ESL-school program.

"English only" policy

Schools that allow students to speak their native language on-site quickly develop a bad reputation among the international-student population. In general, students want to be forced to break the habit of resorting to their own language to communicate effectively. Many schools have strict "English only" policies whereby students may lose school computer privileges or even be expelled if they are caught using their native language. Schools that do not have strict policies are often the object of ridicule in ESL chat rooms and weblogs. Some students choose not to attend schools that do not enforce an "English only" rule.

SAMPLE 1
TYPICAL ESL-SCHOOL PROGRAM

Full-time ESL Program (General)
English Basics: Monday to Friday, 9:00 a.m.–12:00 p.m. Levels: Beginner, Intermediate, Advanced Course content: • Grammar • Vocabulary building • Speaking • Listening • Reading • Writing • Pronunciation Electives: Monday to Thursday, 1:00 p.m.–4:00 p.m. Levels: Beginner, Intermediate, Advanced Elective choices: • Conversation • Idioms and Slang • Academic English • Business English • TOEFL • TOEIC

Types of locations

Most international schools are located in large urban centers. In the United States, cities such as Los Angeles, Austin, New York, and Chicago attract thousands of international students each year. Students who choose to study in Canada most often opt for Toronto or Vancouver. Most international students come from large cities in their home country and are therefore more comfortable in busy urban centers that have an exciting nightlife, shopping malls, public transportation, and easy access to an international airport.

However, the trend toward small towns is growing. Many students — especially those who have been studying in cities for several months — are discovering that small towns offer a cleaner, safer, and friendlier environment in which to learn English. In small towns, there are fewer opportunities to meet people who speak Hindi, Korean, Chinese, or

Japanese. Students are, therefore, forced to use English more often.

It can be a hard sell getting students to accept the idea of going to a small town. But it is possible, if you can find out what the larger centers are lacking and capitalize on it. Vancouver-based students, for instance, complain that there are too many opportunities to use their native language outside of school. They also complain about not being able to make Canadian friends and about being homesick. All three complaints are related, and so is the solution. If students live in a small town where no one speaks their native tongue, they are forced to use English to communicate and, in turn, pick up the language faster. And by being more communicative and confident in their skills, they are more likely to make connections with native English speakers (who sometimes do not have the patience for or interest in befriending people who can barely speak the language and frequently ask for information to be repeated). In the end, the students are more likely to make English-speaking friends and, presumably, have less reason to be homesick.

Small-town schools that market the English-only, family-focused environment of both the school and the community are able to win over students who want a change from the city scene. Also, some parents of younger students are interested in sending their children to smaller, safer communities.

Peak seasons

Many ESL schools offer vacation study programs for school-age children during the summer months. Most often, the programs are four weeks in length and involve both classroom study and outdoor activities.

Many international college and university students choose to study during their vacations too. However, not all school vacations occur at the same time. In South Korea, for example, the post-secondary school year runs from March to December, meaning that students are on vacation in January and February.

Tuition fees

While tuition fees vary from school to school, a typical full-time language program in a well-established institute costs about US$1,300 per month, plus registration fees (approximately US$100). There may also be material fees to consider, as well as extra costs for airport pick-up, activities, and health insurance.

ESL PRODUCTS

ESL schools and tutorial services require ESL products in order to conduct business. They not only need textbooks but also a wide variety of learning materials and resources, such as maps, picture dictionaries, books, flash cards, props, CDs, videotapes and DVDs, and computer programs. Schools and tutorial services may also be in the market for premade curriculum materials, particularly if they are in the early stages of business development. Or they may be looking for everyday items they can use to market their business, such as pens and writing paper printed with the school's logo and contact information.

Once your school or tutorial service is stable, you may want to consider venturing into other industry-related areas. You might decide to create your own textbooks, which will ultimately save your business money on resources. Or you might create, patent, and sell one-month programs to schools overseas. Here are some other cool and unusual products you could use yourself and sell to others.

Classroom props for role plays could include —

- costumes that represent different social or economic roles (e.g., a nurse, a server in a restaurant, a police officer),
- household items in exaggerated sizes made out of cardboard or foam,
- backdrops for skits, and
- traffic signs.

How-to videos and documentaries that demonstrate important aspects of the international-student experience and that are helpful to ESL teachers include —

- how to stay safe in the city,
- student biographies,
- homestay problems and solutions,
- tips on classroom management, and
- ideas for working with students with disabilities.

Promotional materials include —

- calendars featuring pictures of and/or artwork by students,
- clothing and accessories with pictures of and/or artwork by students, and
- video clips of students demonstrating various speaking abilities (to be posted on the school's website).

ESL-related publications include —

- short stories and novels written at levels appropriate to ESL students,
- stories and poems written by ESL students, and
- a newspaper for ESL students.

ENGLISH-ON-THE-GO

A portable ESL business or "English-on-the-go" is another way of developing your ESL business.

With a portable ESL service, you can offer lesson packages to companies, rather than individuals. Industry-specific, on-site English classes may be attractive to business owners who hire foreign-born employees. English classes designed to help staff overcome pronunciation difficulties or better understand customer-service language are a benefit to both the employees and the company.

TEACHER TRAINING

Teacher-training programs are not all created equal. Some are comprehensive university-based programs that last two years. Others run for a week and are designed to quickly prepare "teachers" for work overseas at English institutes. Still others are offered online, allowing prospective teachers to work at their own pace, even in remote places.

There are three main teacher-training courses:

- Teaching English as a Second Language (TESL)
- Teacher of English to Speakers of Other Languages (TESOL)
- Teaching English as a Foreign Language (TEFL)

For the most part, TESL, TESOL, and TEFL amount to the same thing. The difference is in the content they prepare you to teach. For example, TEFL focuses on teaching content designed for students living in their home country, rather than for students who are living and studying in an English-speaking country. Students studying English in their home country are less likely to need help with practical everyday conversation and more likely to need academic or workplace English for the purpose of test preparation.

Teacher training is becoming increasingly competitive. Already, many North American ESL schools have regulations regarding teacher qualifications, making it difficult for new teacher-training organizations to establish credibility. However, there *is* room for teacher training designed for specific types of people planning to travel and teach overseas.

In recent years, there has been a push from industry leaders to create ESL associations that adhere to guidelines and restrictions about teaching credentials. The consensus seems to be that the more time spent studying and practicing teaching, the better equipped the teacher. Of course, whether this is true is debatable and is not at issue here. (Indeed, on more than one occasion I have witnessed irreparable damage done in schools by teachers with amazing credentials and decades of experience.) What is important is that if you start an ESL-teacher-training business, your students could have difficulty getting their credential recognized if your program does not meet the current, yet ever-changing, industry standards.

In some cases, credential recognition is not an issue. For example, you can offer teacher-training programs to international students planning to teach English when they return to their home country. Or your program could be designed for North Americans hoping to make some money while traveling in other countries.

ESL SERVICES

When it comes to extra ESL services, there is a wide range of options to choose from. The trick is to find out what services are missing in your own business and in your area. A more complex approach is to create a need in your clientele.

Since international students live overseas for a significant period of time, you may want to start by thinking about what they need, use, and do in their daily lives. For example, since many students relocate more than once during their overseas stay, you may want to offer relocation services, including transportation and muscle to help move belongings and/or furniture. Indeed, even a transportation service has the potential for success in areas where students have limited options.

Or, knowing that students often feel homesick and disoriented, you may want to provide special counseling or mentoring services. On a related note, you could make students feel more at home by opening a lunchtime catering service featuring food from their home countries. Since so many students travel during their overseas study period, you could form partnerships with hotel or bed-and-breakfast owners in neighboring cities and offer "travel and learn" programs.

Corporations also make use of ESL services. You could build and sell ESL-based customer-service programs to companies that hire non-native English speakers. Many large hotels and restaurant chains rely on foreign-born staff who might benefit from classes in listening, reading, writing, and of course speaking and pronunciation. Offering to help a company help its employees improve customer service might win over the management.

HOMESTAY

While homestay services may already be part of the overall plan for your school or tutorial service, you may want to consider expanding the business and offering your accommodation services to other institutions.

Some cities have homestay businesses that cater to a variety of colleges and universities. The institution hires the homestay organization to take care of everything from homestay assessment to student placement to airport pickup to management of funds.

The homestay organization makes money from student fees, such as the registration fee, the pickup fee, the change of homestay fee, and a percentage of students' monthly fees. For example, a student might pay $700 per month in homestay fees. The homestay organization might keep $50, passing the remaining $650 on to the homestay family.

The homestay business is not for everyone. People with strong organizational skills, well-developed interpersonal skills, and patience are best suited for the job, as the work is people-centered and often involves coping with individuals' feelings and emotions.

WHICH ESL OPTION IS RIGHT FOR YOU?

The ESL industry is a new sector in the economy, and there is a great deal of room for growth, development, and change. With the right people, the right plan, and the right attitude (i.e., the "student as customer" philosophy), the opportunities are limitless.

Before continuing on in this book, spend a few moments considering your background and work style, and then take the suitability test in Exercise 1. This test is designed to help you figure out which business option is best for you — an ESL tutorial service or an ESL school.

Regardless of the results, you should read through all the chapters in this book *before* making a final decision and starting to do the exercises designed for one of the two major business options.

Good luck!

PART 1 EXERCISES

Exercise 1
Suitability Test

Write down the number from one to ten that best reflects your answers to each of the questions below. Add up your answers and check your results against the results key.

1. How familiar are you with the ESL industry?
   - 0 = New to the ESL industry
   - 5 = Less than five years of experience
   - 10 = More than ten years of experience
   - Score: _0_

2. How much experience do you have working (teaching or other) in private ESL schools?
   - 0 = None
   - 5 = Five years
   - 10 = Lots of experience in many different schools
   - Score: _0_

3. Have you tutored ESL students before?
   - 0 = No
   - 5 = Yes, children only
   - 10 = Yes, children and adults
   - Score: _0_

4. Are you an introvert or an extrovert?
   - 0 = An introvert
   - 5 = A bit of both
   - 10 = An extrovert
   - Score: _5_

5. How would you rank your communication and interpersonal skills?
   - 0 = Not sure
   - 5 = Better one-on-one than in groups
   - 10 = Comfortable with individuals and large groups
   - Score: _5_

6. How would you prefer to work?
   - 0 = Not sure
   - 5 = Alone, from home
   - 10 = Outside the home, with a team of people
   - Score: _5_

7. How would you rate your organizational skills?

    0 = I need to work on them

    5 = Fairly strong if I'm not overloaded

    10 = Exceptional

    Score: 10

8. How would you describe your people-management skills?

    0 = No management experience

    5 = Good, if it's a small group

    10 = Strong, whether it's a small group or a large group

    Score: 5

9. Are you a financial risk taker?

    0 = No, taking risks terrifies me

    5 = Sometimes, but I'm usually careful

    10 = I'm not afraid to take risks

    Score: 5

10. How would you rate your financial experience?

    0 = I never balance my checkbook

    5 = I track my personal finances

    10 = I have run a business before

    Score: 5

Total Score: 40 /100

Results Key

If you scored between 10 and 40:

Because you have limited experience in the ESL industry, you might want to consider finding a business partner(s) with significant industry experience.

If you scored between 41 and 60:

You are probably best suited to starting and running an ESL tutorial service.

If you scored between 61 and 84:

You are probably best suited to starting and running an ESL school.

If you scored between 85 and 100:

Take your pick! You are likely to succeed at either venture.

Part 2

STARTING AND RUNNING AN ESL TUTORIAL SERVICE

Chapter 3

UNDERSTANDING YOUR ROLE
IN THE ESL-TUTORING MARKET

Hiring a tutor is a way for new immigrants and international students in public and private school systems to get ahead. With its personalized lessons and one-on-one attention, tutoring works for people from all walks of life, from the newly landed young person struggling to keep up with his or her middle-school classmates to the adult student needing a crash course in TOEFL in order to enter a North American post-secondary institution. Immigrant parents of young children hire language tutors and homework helpers, as do international graduate students and business-people with money available for language lessons or assistance with the writing or editing of documents and essays.

In Asia and many other parts of the world, hiring a tutor for help in English (and math and science) is common practice. When students come to North America to study English at a private ESL school or college, some hire conversation tutors to enhance their classroom performance. Students who have only a limited amount of time overseas might need one-on-one expert help in specific areas such as business English, TOEFL, or TOEIC. Some students even choose to attend classes part time, devoting the remainder of their time to private lessons and self-study.

Affluent parents of university-bound immigrant youth often send their children to after-school institutions that offer personalized academic help. Some seek out tutorial services that have tutors who conduct lessons in students' homes.

A recent trend in the industry is to provide ESL services to international students with special needs, such as a physical impairment or even social and emotional issues that make participation in a typical ESL classroom difficult or overwhelming.

EXPLORING YOUR MARKET

In order to determine what kind of tutorial service you are going to operate, you need to explore your market options. First, find out what kind of ESL students live and study in your area. Are they international students preparing for university or college in North America? Are they visitors looking for a few months of overseas fun and conversation with native English speakers? Are they new immigrants who have children struggling in the English-based school system?

You also need to find out how many students in your area come from countries that understand and value personalized language instruction. How many students hired tutors in their home country? More important, how many would be willing to pay for such services overseas?

Another consideration is the expectations of the students. What kind of tutorial arrangement are the students accustomed to? Do they prefer a formal arrangement that is signed and sealed in contract form or an informal agreement, with flexibility in terms of times, location, and even payment schedule? What kind of tutorial facility are they expecting — an official tutorial-business site? a public place, such as a library or a café? the tutor's home? the student's home?

Understanding students' expectations regarding money is also important. How much do students expect to pay for tutorial services? And what do they expect to be covered by that fee — textbooks? photocopied materials? a ride to and from the tutorial site? coffee and/or snacks?

The more you can find out about what students expect, the better you can plan how you will meet their needs.

FINDING A NICHE MARKET

Now that you have a clear picture of your market, it is time to make decisions regarding your operation. Are you planning to have an official location, equipped with tutorial rooms and set hours of operation? Or are you going to go the more portable route, with a website and telephone number as contact information, and a variety of location choices available to students, such as their home, your home, and the library?

Part of your decision should be based on where you see a gap in the market. If your area already has an established tutorial service that serves the after-school immigrant market, you might want to offer parents an alternative setup with flexible hours and more personalized service. Or you might simply pursue the international student market.

On a similar note, if your area does not have a formal tutorial service, but instead features a loose network of people willing to tutor, you might want to establish a formal business that unites them under one umbrella.

Finding your niche requires legwork. The first step is finding out what is missing in your area. You then need to talk to prospective students about the options they would like to have. For example, there may be a need for evening or weekend tutoring. Or perhaps international students would make good use of a drop-in center.

Keeping an eye out for new and emerging markets — such as international students with disabilities or immigrants running businesses who have shaky English skills — will also help you stay competitive.

Chapter  4

DEVELOPING YOUR PROGRAMS
AND SERVICES

Whether you have chosen to open a formal tutorial service for immigrant youth, an informal tutor network for adult international students, or a combination of education services, your programs and services must match the needs, desires, and expectations of your clientele. Your programs and services also need to be easily understood by your target market.

Tutoring programs differ from school programs in that they are created to suit the specific needs of a particular individual. The actual tutorial program cannot really begin until *after* the student is assessed and interviewed about his or her strengths and weaknesses, short-term and long-term goals, and areas of interest. However, the system of tutorial delivery can and should be developed before students access your services. In short, before you open your doors (or telephone lines), you need to set up an assessment system and a schedule outlining program-delivery options. Making decisions about assessments and program delivery requires some big-picture planning.

BIG PICTURE PLANNING

To market your services effectively, you need to be able to describe your business concept and the services you offer in a sentence or two. You should also be able to answer questions about details when necessary.

Clarifying your business concept and services requires the following:

- Creating a student profile (or profiles, if you are serving more than one type of client)

- Determining the purpose of your program through a mission statement

- Clarifying your delivery methods

- Defining your market niche

- Outlining your programs and services

- Creating a system of evaluation

Creating a student profile

The types of services you offer will depend on the types of students you have. Are they immigrant children, students from overseas attending high school, adult international students, or recent immigrants in the workforce? Do they attend school during the day and require extra help at night, or are they free during regular business hours? Do they have special needs and therefore require special services?

Sample 2 provides an example of a student profile.

Determining the purpose of your program through a mission statement

The key to big picture planning is to clarify your school's purpose. Consider the following questions:

- What do you aim to accomplish with your services?

- What do you strive to provide to your students?

- What do you hope your students will be able to do when they complete the training you offer?

- What makes your services different from those offered by other tutorial services?

In short, what is your mission statement?

For example, suppose you decide to target the students described in the student profile in Sample 2. You know that these students are more interested in gaining confidence through the overseas experience than in working hard

SAMPLE 2
PROFILE OF STUDENTS

Profile of 123 Tutoring Services Students

- Teenagers or in early 20s

- From Asia

- At-risk youth (have dropped out of school and/or are having problems fitting into the regular school system) or have special needs (visually impaired, physically challenged)

- Want overseas English experience but can't find a school to accommodate their needs and goals

- Plan to study overseas for six months

- Want to learn English in a low-pressure environment

- Hope to build confidence and social skills through development of oral English skills

---

to improve their academic performance. You also know that your market does not fit into the regular school system and therefore prefers to have flexibility with regards to lesson content, delivery, and lesson times. Therefore, you might have a mission statement similar to the one in Sample 3.

Clarifying your delivery method

With your mission statement in place, your next step is to clarify how you plan to make good on your promises. How will you ensure that your study times stay flexible? How many and what kind of tutors do you need to hire in order to deliver unique, custom-designed tutorials?

For instance, let us imagine that your services target at-risk youth and students with special needs. You will likely need to draw from a pool of tutors who display great patience and are willing to work flexible hours. Your tutors will also need to have strong interpersonal skills and be able to read people well. Skilled tutors who specialize in working with people who have special needs would be particularly helpful. Lastly, your employees (or contractors) need to be able to think on their feet. They should be able to quickly and accurately assess a student's needs, abilities, and goals, and be able to create a tutorial plan that matches the student's profile.

For the business described above, the methodology description might look like the one in Sample 4.

SAMPLE 3
TUTORING MISSION STATEMENT

---

123 Tutoring Services Mission Statement

At 123 Tutoring Services, we aim to help students with unique challenges achieve their English-communication goals by offering a wide range of custom-designed lessons and flexible study times.

SAMPLE 4
METHODOLOGY DESCRIPTION

---

123 Tutoring Services Methodology Description

123 Tutoring Services offers —
- custom-designed programs that help students develop confidence and English-communication skills.

Our tutors are —
- trained professionals available to teach mornings, afternoons, evenings, and weekends.

Our tutorials are held —
- in the location that best fits the needs of each student — the student's home, a tutorial room, the library, a community center, or any other meeting place the student chooses.

Defining how your services fill a market niche

In Chapter 3, you had an opportunity to think of things that make your services special or in some way different from those of your competitors. Articulating your uniqueness clearly and concisely will help you create marketing materials that grab the attention of your target market.

In the case of 123 Tutoring Services, for example, the most unique feature is the market itself. Few schools or tutoring companies focus on helping at-risk ESL learners, and even fewer are specifically designed for those with physical challenges. Students who fit these descriptions would want to know that they are not only welcome at 123 Tutoring Services, but that they are preferred clientele. Letting them know means creating marketing materials that highlight these points.

Sample 5 outlines the "marketing promise" for 123 Tutoring Services.

Outlining your programs and services

Turning to practical matters, your next step is creating a schedule that shows potential customers what your programs and services are and when they are available. Because the schedule will be used for marketing purposes, the information should be clearly laid out and easy for second-language learners to understand.

The schedule should include information on specific programs. For example, you might offer an after-school program for public school students, an academic English program for university-bound international students, or a "study buddy" conversation program where two students work with one tutor. Your schedule should also include hours of operation and fees, and any related services and activities you offer (e.g., transportation and accommodation services and extracurricular activities).

Because tutorials are typically one-on-one sessions, a "program" can last as many weeks

SAMPLE 5
MARKETING PROMISE

---

123 Tutoring Services Marketing Promise

At 123 Tutoring Services, we guarantee —

- a warm, friendly, low-pressure learning environment;
- individual and small-group instruction from caring professionals;
- custom-designed ESL lessons and flexible schedules that match each student's needs, goals, and lifestyle; and
- our commitment to welcoming and accommodating every type of student, whether physically challenged or in need of special attention and care, to ensure that each student succeeds in his or her learning endeavors.

---

or months as a student wants. Programs that have more than one student in a session may have start and end dates. Smaller operations, with a varied market but limited tutor availability, may want to reserve certain parts of the workday for a specific type of customer. For example, the 3:00 p.m. to 6:00 p.m. period may be reserved for public school students.

Normally, tutorial services are designed to accommodate any level of student. However, not all tutors are comfortable working with students at every level. To ensure a comfortable match, you may need to develop a student-assessment system that identifies a student's strengths and weaknesses in English. Having information about a student's language abilities can help a tutor better prepare to work with the student.

Assessment systems can be found in textbooks and on websites. You can also create your own signature assessment system, with your own brand of coding and criteria (see the next section, "Establishing an intake and assessment system," for more information).

While some tutorial services have set times for specific programs (e.g., Academic Preparation in the evenings, Monday to Wednesday), many businesses keep their program times relatively flexible. What they monitor carefully, however, is their hours of operation. Smaller companies with fewer tutors available might only be open for business four or five days a week, but for 12 to 14 hours a day. For example, tutoring might be available from 7:00 a.m. to 9:00 p.m., Wednesday through Saturday. Larger organizations with more staff are more likely to be open seven days a week.

Another thing that needs to be considered is travel time during the peak hours of the day. In small towns, commuting time is rarely an issue: tutors can move from one student's home to another quickly. But in large urban centers, traveling during rush hour can be a nightmare. However, if a tutorial service has a fixed location, the onus is on the students to brave the traffic and be on time.

When developing your schedule information, ensure that your tutorial options and times are clearly coded and easy for language learners to read. Also include information about the other services you offer. For example, if you know your target market is interested in developing both language skills and social skills, you might offer a range of tutoring options, plus fun guided tours and activities that encourage communication between students and native English speakers. In addition to services designed to attract students with attendance issues and/or physical challenges, you could offer transportation and even accommodation.

Sample 6 is an example of a services schedule.

Establishing an intake and assessment system

Once you know what programs and services you will be offering, you need to set up a method of intake and assessment that allows students to access your services and find the right tutorial match.

In both large and small tutoring businesses, the intake procedure might consist of an interview or "consultation" that establishes a student's level, goals, needs, preferences, availability for sessions, and budget. During the consultation, the student would be given information about tutors, programs and services, and schedules.

SAMPLE 6
TUTORING SERVICES SCHEDULE

123 Tutoring Services Schedule	
Tutoring	Guided Tours and Activities
Monday to Thursday 9:00 a.m.–9:00 p.m. $25–$35 per hour	Friday to Sunday 9:00 a.m.–9:00 p.m. $15–$50 per student, depending on the activity
Optional Services • Transportation: $50 per month • Accommodation: $650 per month	

In terms of tutoring, defining a student's level is necessary for two reasons. First, some students (as well as many parents) are eager to monitor the linear progress of their language abilities. (After all, hiring a tutor can be expensive, and most customers want to see results.) Second, some tutors are uncomfortable tutoring students with certain ability levels, and a mismatch can do more harm than you might expect since unhappy students may tell other students about their experiences.

While not always necessary, keeping records of the "start and end" levels of every student has other benefits. For instance, students who progress exceptionally well can become walking advertisements, living proof that your services have value and produce results. With this in mind, you might want to devise entrance and exit assessments that can be compared to each other. Monthly or periodic assessments are also appreciated by students who are concerned about their progress and need help identifying the areas in which they need the most help.

Your evaluation system should be generic, meaning that it shouldn't incorporate the program content designed for a particular student. However, the system should be designed so that it evaluates measurable skills, such as reading comprehension and speaking ability. What you'll need to do is define each assessment level.

Perhaps the easiest way to define the levels is to use a premade assessment "test," such as those featured in grammar textbooks and websites. Another option is to follow a formal system that uses a videotaped interview and a writing assignment that are assessed according to grammar levels described in a grammar text. The results are later compared to the results from an exit assessment.

A simpler system, ideal for smaller, less formal tutorial services, is to have a student read and answer questions about a short newspaper article (newspapers are typically written at an 8th Grade or middle-school level, and are therefore somewhat advanced for the ESL learner). A student who cannot manage the vocabulary in the heading and lead paragraph might be deemed Beginner (or Level 2, or whatever terminology you have decided to use). A student who can understand the words but not the real meaning of the article might be an Intermediate student. And a student who can understand most of the vocabulary and can talk about the subject discussed in the article might be an Advanced student. Samples 7 and 8 show some examples of assessment tools.

Whichever system you use, the important thing is to ensure that the entrance results can be fairly compared to the exit results. The other thing to keep in mind is your target market. If your target market is the academic, bookish type, they will likely appreciate the kind of assessment system that resembles their destination — college or university. If your target market is looking for an alternative to the academic setting, they will probably be

SAMPLE 7
AEIOU LEVEL ASSESSMENT

---

123 Tutoring Services AEIOU Level Assessment

About me (shows knowledge of simple present, present progressive)

- Occupation
- Interests
- Family

Experiences (shows knowledge of simple past, present, and past perfect)

- Work
- Relationships
- Travel

Information (shows knowledge of gerunds and infinitives, passive)

- Culture
- Business and industry
- News

Opinions (shows knowledge of conditionals, quoted/reported speech)

- Politics
- Religion
- Social policy

University preparation (academic reading and writing ability, advanced vocabulary)

- Science
- Literature
- Argument/presentation skills

SAMPLE 8
LEVEL ASSESSMENT FORM

123 Tutoring Services Level Assessment Form

Name:_____ Interview date:_____

Part 1   Notes:

Vocabulary   /10

Pronunciation   /10

Expressions   /10

Confidence   /10

Part 2   Notes:

Grammar   /20

Listening   /20

Writing   /20

Scoring

Part 1:   /40

Part 2:   /60

Total: /100

Level (circle one):   1   2   3

Estimated time for each AEIOU section:_____ hours

---

more comfortable with a less intimidating, more low-pressure type of assessment system.

As an example, suppose your mandate and target market are similar to those of 123 Tutoring Services — custom-designed ESL programs for at-risk youth and students with physical challenges. Your assessment system is likely to be relatively informal, with an emphasis on speaking and listening. The content of both your entrance and exit assessments would likely be familiar topics that are easy to discuss. You would measure oral grammar skills, keeping in mind the student's confidence level. Sample 9 is what the assessment might look like in a case like this.

When it comes to evaluating students, be warned: students with limited English skills are sometimes sensitive (and even defensive) about being categorized as a beginner-level student. If your target market is not academic and therefore not interested in having a score to improve upon, you might want to devise a

SAMPLE 9
ENTRANCE AND EXIT ASSESSMENT SYSTEM

---

123 Tutoring Services Assessment System

Use this assessment system when a student is entering the program and exiting it, and compare the two scores.

Technique

- Videotaped or audiotaped interview response to, "Tell me about yourself."

Terms of assessment

- Examiner listens for a variety of oral skills: vocabulary level, pronunciation, use of idioms and expressions, comfort level, and fluency.
- Student is assessed based on the AEIOU grammar and given a mark out of 100.

---

system that de-emphasizes traditional labels. However, if your students require or request more tangible evidence of improvement, you will need a system that features terms or figures indicating progression.

PROGRAM AND SERVICE OPTIONS

Now that you have created a big-picture vision of your ESL tutorial business, you need to flesh out the information on your programs and services by adding details about tutoring methods and materials, as well as service options and accessibility. The information should be written in a way that is easy for new staff and prospective students to understand.

There are two main types of tutoring: content-based tutoring and student-led tutoring. In content-based tutoring, the tutor collects and organizes information and learning materials and delivers these to the student. During a session, the student receives instruction and, when applicable, is given homework

assignments related to the lesson. The tutor may even provide the student with the material that will be covered in the next lesson, giving the learner time to prepare for the lesson ahead of time.

In student-led tutoring the student is responsible for the content and direction of the lesson. During each session, the student raises questions (e.g., how to understand and use a tough grammar point, or how to politely bring up a problem with a homestay host) or topics for discussion (e.g., a recent news item or a confusing cultural difference that is causing him or her concern). The student may ask the tutor to help him or her read and understand a newspaper article, correct a collection of sentences using new vocabulary words, or simply assist with a homework assignment.

Because content-based tutoring requires extra time and work in terms of preparing and organizing materials, you may want to charge more for programs that use this method. That said, while student-led tutoring is less demanding in terms of preparation, some instructors find it more difficult precisely because they cannot prepare for what they may be asked or are expected to know.

Both content-based and student-led tutoring methods can be used for almost any type of program, with any level, type, or age of student. You may want to offer your students both options. Or, you could insist on using content-based instruction for certain types of programs, the most obvious being grammar or TOEFL lessons, and use student-led tutoring for lighter, less rule-oriented types of programs.

When deciding on your tutoring methods and materials, you will need to consider your target market's needs, desires, and expectations, while keeping in mind the nature of your facilities. If you are setting up a formal location, you will have more options, since some tutors could be available on-site while others are working at students' homes.

Program options for immigrant youth

If your primary market is immigrant youth needing help with schoolwork, your programs might simply be assistance with homework assignments (student-led) and extra lessons in a student's area of weakness (content-based). The program could be called Homework Help, and services could include transportation to and/or from the tutoring facility. You could also offer a home-tutoring option for parents who prefer to have their children close by.

If your facility is large enough, you may want to give students the choice of working one-on-one with a tutor or, for a lower rate, being part of a small group. In such a setup, language-related books and other useful learning materials (e.g., maps, globes, picture dictionaries, computers that are connected to the Internet) could be made available to tutors and students.

Catering to the school-age market means your tutors would work in the before-school and after-school periods, in the evenings, and on weekends. During seasonal breaks such as summer and winter holidays, your services could be available during the day. You could even develop special vacation programs, which would compete with other educational and adventure-related "camps" that children attend when they are not in school.

Program options for adult international students

If your primary market is adult international students, you might offer a range of content-based and student-led academic and social programs. Students with specific academic goals in mind could opt for a tutor who specializes in a popular academic area (e.g., Academic Preparation, TOEFL, Essay Writing), while students interested in business could choose a TOEIC or Business English tutor. For those needing help with everyday English communication, there could be tutors in Everyday Conversation, Idioms and Slang, or even a combination of the above.

There are numerous books and resources available to tutors working with academic students. For test-based programs such as the TOEFL, tutors may simply follow a tried-and-true textbook that includes practice tests and audio CDs. Or they may use textbooks and learning materials that have grammar and vocabulary-building exercises, taped news segments for listening practice, or other helpful materials that will prepare students for the reading comprehension section of the TOEFL.

For students interested only in improving their conversation skills, you could offer both one-on-one and small-group conversation tutorials. Sample 10 provides two examples of student-led methods of tutoring conversation.

See Sample 11 for a handout tutors can provide to students for the preparation of their Wish Club communication sessions. You can evaluate students using the form in Sample 12.

Extracurricular program options for all ages and types of students

In addition to academic or language-based programs, you could offer a range of alternative programs aimed at enhancing students' social skills and/or promoting their physical well-being. Depending on the size and scope of your operation and your target market's interests and desires, each week or month, students could be offered a choice of activities and given the option of signing up for them. Activities could include the following:

- Field trips to interesting landmarks or areas of the city
- Art or dance classes
- Guided adventure tours — biking, hiking, rock climbing, canoeing
- Shopping tours in a neighboring town
- Camping trips
- Sports day and picnic
- Book or poetry readings
- Movie night — watch and discuss a movie
- Fact-finding mission or treasure hunt

See Sample 13 for some program ideas.

ORGANIZING AND SCHEDULING

Regardless of the size and complexity of your operation, you (and your team of tutors and staff, if applicable) are going to need an organizational system to ensure that you have all your ducks in a row at all times. Both large and small operations are wise to have a central booking person who is responsible for matching students with tutors and distributing new-student orientation packages that contain some of the following information about your organization:

- Programs and services
- Expectations of students and tutors
- Maps
- Local transportation system
- Landmarks of interest
- Any other "welcome" documents you choose to include

Your booking person may also keep track of start and end times of lessons, schedule changes, and fee arrangements.

In order to match a student with a tutor, your booking person needs the following information about the student:

- English level
- Study interests
- Hours of availability
- Desired number of tutorial hours per week
- Preferred study style and method

The easiest way to collect this information is to create a contract that acts as both an interview and an assessment form. Through the process of providing information about program and fee options, and getting to know the student's background and study interests, the booking person will get a general sense of the student's speaking and listening skills. However, a more precise level assessment should be done in order to measure the student's reading comprehension and writing skills (see the section on assessment earlier in this chapter).

Once the booking person locates a tutor who fulfills the requirements of the student, all three parties — the booking person, the tutor, and the student — sign an agreement, or contract, outlining the following:

- Student's contact information
- Tutor's contact information
- Lesson start and end dates
- Lesson location and times
- Student's level, study interests, and goals
- Payment schedule

- Late penalties and cancellation policy if applicable

Sample 14 is an example of a tutorial contract.

Many tutors also find it useful to give a lesson summary to the parents of children in public school. This detailed form serves two purposes: it acts as a log of the activities done with the student, as well as an invoice for the parents.

Sample 15 provides an example of a lesson summary.

Since most tutors work with more than one student in a given month, they, too, need to stay organized. An easy way to keep track of students and work hours is for the tutor to map out his or her schedule on a calendar in pencil (see Sample 16). After each session is completed, the tutor retraces the student's name and hours worked with a felt pen, making it easy to calculate how many hours he or she worked in a given week or month.

SAMPLE 10
STUDENT-LED METHODS OF TUTORING CONVERSATION

Build-a-Book Method (for one-on-one tutorials)

The build-a-book method is designed for students aiming for error-free oral communication skills at native-English-speaker speed. The idea is to help the student create a notebook full of anecdotes, ideas, and expressions that are both practical and meaningful to the student in terms of future communication in English-speaking environments. The student talks about himself or herself and his or her interests while the tutor corrects the student's pronunciation and grammar and records the accurate version in the notebook. After each lesson, the student can practice, using the notes provided, in preparation for the next session.

The following is an overview of the six steps used to "build a book."

1. Ask the student to bring a ringed notebook to the session. Tell the student that he or she will be talking while you are correcting and writing.

2. During each session, use the notebook to record the corrected version of the sentences and expressions used during the student's conversation.

Example:

The student says, "I live in Powell River since two months." Correct the student verbally, and record the sentence in the notebook: "I have lived in Powell River for two months." The student can then study and practice the corrected version of the conversation at home.

3. Designate pages for pronunciation errors and corrections. Review regularly.

4. Designate pages for new vocabulary. Test the student regularly.

5. Designate pages for slang and idioms, if applicable.

6. Use the notebook for regular review sessions. Flip through and ask the student questions about past sessions. Give review tests.

Wish Club Method (for pairs or small-group tutorials)

Wish Club, which comes from the name "world issues club," is designed to help students with weak communication skills learn how to start and maintain a conversation. The idea is to prepare students for conversations in social settings with native English speakers. Students are required to prepare a one-page handout containing information about a current event of their choice, a list of new and challenging vocabulary words or expressions, and a series of questions to ask the other members of the group. Students are given 30 minutes to present the information, teach the new words, and manage a conversation based on the questions they prepared. The tutor's role is to observe and listen to each student lead a conversation and to record comments and suggestions regarding problem areas in terms of pronunciation, grammar, content, and style. At the end of each Wish Club presentation, or "communication session," the tutor briefly goes over the comments with the student, congratulating him or her on the strong elements of the session and pointing out ways to improve for the next Wish Club meeting.

HANDOUT FOR WISH CLUB COMMUNICATION SESSIONS

What is a communication session?

A communication session is a 30-minute student-led conversation based on a world issue, event, or trend that the student finds interesting.

At every Wish Club meeting, each student is required to —

- provide the other students with information about a topic,
- introduce and explain new vocabulary, and
- ask/answer questions about the topic.

How do I prepare?

1. Consider the issues, trends, and events taking place in the news right now.
2. Choose a topic that interests you.
3. Prepare a one-page handout that includes —
   - information,
   - five new vocabulary words, and
   - three or more discussion questions.
4. Practice presenting your topic, keeping in mind that your goal is to introduce a topic and keep the conversation flowing.

Where do I find resources?

You can draw on a variety of resources:

- Newspapers, magazines, books
- The Internet
- Song lyrics
- Something you have written

WISH CLUB COMMUNICATION SESSIONS EVALUATION FORM

Student's name_____ Date_____

Topic_____

Content:

/10

Pronunciation:

/10

Grammar:

/10

Conversation management:

/10

Total score: /40

PROGRAMS AND SERVICES

123 Tutoring Services: Customized ESL Programs and Outdoor Adventures

ESL Programs

One-on-one tutoring	$25–$40 per hour
Small-group tutoring	(varies depending on group size, materials and preparation time, and whether transportation is required)

Program Options:

Everyday Conversation	Academic English
TOEFL/TOEIC	Business English
Job-Search English	Current Events
Writing	Other:_____

Location Options:

123 Tutoring Services site	Student's home
Tutor's home	Other:_____

Time Options: Monday to Thursday between 9:00 a.m. and 9:00 p.m.

Guided Adventure Tours and Activities

One-on-one	$10–$30 per hour
Small group	(varies depending on group size, materials and preparation time, and whether transportation is required)

Tour and Activity Options:

Rock climbing	Scuba diving
Hiking	Canoeing
Kayaking	Other:_____

Time Options: Friday to Sunday between 9:00 a.m. and 9:00 p.m.

SAMPLE 14
TUTORIAL CONTRACT

Student's name_____

Phone number_____

E-mail_____

Tutor's name_____

Phone number_____

E-mail_____

Meeting place_____

Days and Times	Mon.	Tues.	Wed.	Thurs.	Fri.	Sat.	Sun.
	____	____	____	____	____	____	____

Lesson Details (check all that apply)

[ ] Speaking   [ ] Reading

[ ] Listening   [ ] Writing

[ ] Pronunciation   [ ] Vocabulary

[ ] Idioms/slang   [ ] Grammar

Fee: $_____ per hour

Start date_____   End date_____

Payment

• Students must pay two weeks in advance.

Late Policy

• Session times are not flexible. Even if a student is late, the session will end at the originally scheduled time.

Cancellations

• If a student wishes to cancel a session, he or she must inform the tutor at least two hours before the session begins.

• For sessions cancelled with adequate notice, one make-up session can be scheduled per two-week period.

• A refund will not be given in the case of a cancellation made less than two hours before the scheduled session.

Signed by:

Tutor_____ Student_____ Date_____

SAMPLE 15
LESSON SUMMARY
(for parents of children in public schools)

Lesson Summary
April 1–30, 20--

Hyo Ju Nam (Grade 8 student)
ESL/Homework help

April 1, 3:30–5:00 p.m.   1.5 hours
1. Introduced newspaper article about local high school student
    - Scanned for theme, main ideas
    - New vocabulary: identified, discussed, used in sentences
    - Read aloud for pronunciation
    - Discussion: compared to life of a student in Korea
    - Reviewed notes
2. Discussed schedule, payment, next lesson

April 2, 3:30–4:30 p.m.   1 hour
1. Timed writing (15 min.): paragraph about arrival in the US
    - Discussed areas of weakness (punctuation; run-on sentences; conjunctions)
    - Brief expressions/grammar review (e.g., "will" vs. "be + going to")
2. Correct-the-errors exercise
    - Rewrote flawed sentences
    - Discussed answers

April 8, 3:30–5:00 p.m.   1.5 hours
1. Timed writing (15 min.): paragraph on ski trip to Mount Washington
    - Discussed areas of weakness (prepositions; verb tenses)
    - Brief grammar review (past perfect)
2. Vocabulary building
    - Identified/discussed new words in Mt. Baker ski advertisement
3. Corrected/discussed last session's rewrite

April 10, 3:30–5:00 p.m.   1.5 hours
1. English homework: eagle project
    - Found information on Internet
    - Identified key categories and discussed new vocabulary
2. Timed writing (15 min.): paragraph on a friend's personality
    - Discussed new vocabulary (adjectives that describe personality traits)

April 15, 3:30–5:00 p.m.   1.5 hours
1. Opinions/comparisons: marriage and family structure
   - Identified and discussed various forms of family structures
   - Highlighted key terms and new vocabulary
2. Vocabulary building: personality traits (continued)
   - Used personals ads to identify ten traits
   - Discussed and practiced using new words

April 16, 3:45–5:15 p.m.   1.5 hours
1. Grammar: unreal conditionals
   - Discussed and answered "What would you do if …" questions
   - Identified new words
   - Practiced "If I were_____, I would_____."
2. Idioms/expressions: relationships
   - Discussed high school relationships and dating culture

April 17, 3:30–5:00 p.m.   1.5 hours
1. Timed writing (20 min.): high school relationships
   - Wrote paragraph
   - Identified and discussed spelling/grammar errors
   - Discussed theme and issues
2. Figures of speech: animal idioms
   - Multiple-choice "test"
   - Discussed answers

April 23, 3:30–5:00 p.m.   1.5 hours
1. Vocabulary building/recreating events: health and safety
   - Read and discussed information on West Nile virus
   - Identified new vocabulary
   - Discussed general health issues (e.g., diet, lifestyle, safety)
   - Shared stories about illnesses, injuries

April 24, 3:30–5:00 p.m.   1.5 hours
1. Timed writing (20 min.): health (continued from yesterday's discussion)
   - Wrote paragraph
   - Identified and discussed spelling/grammar errors
2. Using a thesaurus
   - Looked up some commonly used words
   - Discussed and practiced using synonyms listed in the thesaurus

Total: 13 hours at $25 per hour = $325

SAMPLE 16
TUTOR'S SCHEDULE

Tutor's name: Marlie Percival   Program: various

	Monday	Tuesday	Wednesday	Thursday	Friday	Saturday	Sunday	Hours
Week 1	You Jin 9–11 sh Wish Club 3–5 os	Albert 10–1 th	You Jin 9–11 sh Wish Club 3–5 os	Albert 10–1 th		Activity 9–4		21/21
Week 2	You Jin 9–11 sh Wish Club 3–5 os	Albert 10–1 th	You Jin 9–11 sh Wish Club 3–5 os	Albert 10–1 th	Activity 5–9			18/18
Week 3	You Jin 9–11 sh Wish Club 3–5 os	Albert 10–1 th ns	You Jin 9–11 sh Wish Club 3–5 os	Albert 10–1 th	Tour 9–4	Activity 10–8		28/31
Week 4	You Jin 9–11 sh Wish Club 3–5 os	Albert 10–1 th	You Jin 9–11 sh Wish Club 3–5 os	Albert 10–1 th		Activity 9–4	Tour 12–5	26/26

Locations: os (on-site), sh (student's home), th (tutor's home), o (other)

Status: la (late), ns (no show), ca (canceled, with proper notice)

Students: You Jin Ho — Everyday Conversation (12 Red Street, 123-4567)

                    Atsushi Tanaka — Wish Club (34 Blue Street, 789-0123)

                    Hanna Moon — Wish Club (56 Yellow Street, 456-7891)

                    Masumi Yoshioka — Wish Club (78 Green Street, 234-5678)

                    Albert Chin — Academic English/TOEFL (910 Purple Street, 910-1234)

Hours worked: 93   Hours paid: 96

Chapter 5

KEY PEOPLE AND THEIR ROLES

With the right team in place from the beginning, your tutoring business stands a good chance of becoming and staying successful. Early on, you can build a reputation as a tutorial service that delivers what it promises, be it academic programs that enhance students' school performance, conversation programs that improve students' communication skills, outdoor adventure programs that help students learn about and enjoy nature, or a combination of all three.

The "right team" differs according to your business model. A small, academic-tutoring operation may only consist of a lead tutor, who also serves as the coordinator and booking person, and a few energetic tutors willing to work flexible shifts. On the other hand, a large education and adventure service might consist of a program coordinator, a booking person, a number of tutors with a variety of skills, adventure guides, marketing personnel, and even homestay staff.

Small or large, your ESL business needs people who are flexible and comfortable with change. They should also understand the service industry dynamics of the ESL industry, and see students as customers who have a right to make choices about what they are "buying," as well as the right to complain if they receive poor service from a tutor, or are given program materials that do not fit their needs. Have your tutors use Checklist 1 to constantly evaluate whether they are delivering the right service to students.

In larger tutoring businesses, each staff member has a single key role — the program coordinator organizes programs, the booking

CHECKLIST 1
TUTOR SELF-EVALUATION

- ❏ Do you know exactly what the student wants to learn (e.g., practical conversation, topic-based conversation)? Check with the student periodically to make sure he or she still wants to focus on that particular aspect of English.

- ❏ Are you clear about what you expect of the student regarding payments, absentee policy, etc.?

- ❏ Are you sure you understand and agree with what the student expects from you as a tutor (e.g., copies of handouts, snacks, rides, scheduling flexibility)?

- ❏ Are you prepared for change? Students often change their mind about what they want to learn, how they want to learn, and how often they want to meet with a tutor.

- ❏ Are you well organized? Keep a file on each student. Record your students' progress. Keep a record of your hours. Provide receipts for payment if necessary.

- ❏ Are you consistently prepared for teaching and on time for lessons?

- ❏ Many international students hire tutors because their parents tell them to and they may lack self-motivation to learn English. Do you have the patience and skills to help motivate them?

- ❏ When tutoring, it is important to be kind and compliment your students on their progress from time to time. Do you have the temperament to provide positive feedback and reassurance to students who may have difficulty learning English?

person matches students and tutors, the tutors work with students, and so on. In the case of a small tutorial service, however, one person may take on a variety of roles. Then there are one-person operations where the tutor wears the hat of curriculum designer, booking person, marketer, and even bookkeeper.

Regardless of the size and nature of your business at the start-up stage, it is important to understand all the roles that are part of running a tutoring service. After all, over time your business is likely to grow and develop, creating a need for more staff and perhaps a reassignment of roles. Below are some of the key roles in a tutorial service.

PROGRAM COORDINATOR

Your program coordinator is responsible for the smooth delivery of tutorial programs. This means determining which programs should be offered, who should teach them, and which resources tutors should draw from. The program coordinator is the person who tutors talk to about problems with students, materials, or schedules.

A good program coordinator has strong organizational, analytical, and problem-solving skills. The ideal program coordinator would have a university degree and several years of tutoring experience in the private-ESL-school system.

BOOKING PERSON

The booking person's role is to field inquiries from prospective students and initiate the registration process. He or she might explain program information, administer evaluations, and, with the assistance of the program coordinator, match students with tutors, meeting the needs and expectations of the customer.

A booking person organizes the scheduling of tutors and students, as well as managing fee payment. The ideal booking person has strong analytical and organizational skills. The best person for the job is someone who enjoys multitasking and working with people from other countries.

TUTORS

Your tutors are the key to your business's success. Effective ESL tutors have a warm personality and strong interpersonal skills. They are keen listeners who understand that their role as an ESL tutor is to give the student the opportunity to do most of the talking during a given session. Tutors are also good at pacing. That is, they can intuitively sense when it is time to challenge a student, or when it is time to ease off, switch gears, or engage in an activity that makes the student feel positive about his or her progress.

Tutors of English grammar, TOEFL, TOEIC, business English, or any other content-based program, must be knowledgeable about the subject matter and able to communicate this knowledge to students who are at different levels. Good tutors know that one of the keys to student success is confidence. Thus, part of a tutor's role is to boost a student's confidence by being patient and showing enthusiasm and interest in every conversation topic.

Ideally, tutors hold a university degree in an area related to the subjects they are teaching. They would have experience teaching and tutoring international students, and, preferably, experience working overseas. Understanding the role and responsibilities of tutors in other countries, especially in those countries that contain your business's target market, can help a tutor appreciate the level and type of service that students are used to receiving. Having overseas work experience also helps a tutor understand firsthand how disoriented, confused, frustrated, and sometimes depressed a person can become when trying to survive and thrive in a foreign country.

MARKETER

Your marketer is the person who ensures that your community — which includes parents, educators, and the students themselves — knows about your business's products and services. He or she does this by making connections with local and overseas agents, attending education fairs, and networking with schools, parents, and students.

One of the most effective types of marketing is word-of-mouth advertising. Satisfied customers — adult international students or parents of younger students — may do all the advertising you need to make your business successful. (When I ran an informal tutorial service in Vancouver, I never had to advertise after gathering an initial handful of students. The students themselves told their friends about my services, and they told their friends, and so on. For six months, I tutored a variety of students for a total of five or six hours a day.)

Because the marketer deals directly with students as well as international organizations, the ideal person for the job is someone who speaks

English plus at least one of the languages spoken by your target market. Also important are interpersonal skills and the ability to convey the information provided in your business's marketing materials (e.g., website, brochures, and business cards).

Marketers who work for large, formal tutoring businesses need to have a marketing package. A marketing package might contain the following items:

- Program and schedule information
- Blurbs on the tutors and staff
- Homestay and activities information
- Write-ups about the location of the tutorial service and nearby attractions
- Contact information, preferably business cards that include the website and e-mail addresses

Your marketing material and website must look professional if you want students, parents, educators, and agents to take your services seriously. See Chapter 7 for more information on marketing.

ACCOMMODATION COORDINATOR

While some students already have their accommodation arranged by the time they seek tutoring, others may be looking to change homestays or to rent an apartment with a friend. If your tutoring service is small (less than 10 students), you may assist students by checking the newspaper for available suites for rent and making some phone calls on your students' behalf. (You could even build some of the students' lessons around "finding a new place to live," thus helping them help themselves.) If your business is larger and you have many students who need accommodation, you should designate someone to be the accommodation coordinator and have him or her handle all matters related to homestay, apartment-hunting, and moving services.

It is the accommodation coordinator's job to make connections with homestay organizations and/or individual homestay families. The coordinator must also keep an eye on available apartments and know about rental fees and agreements.

Helping students with accommodation requires that the person have good interpersonal skills and great patience. (Students often want to move for reasons that seem picky or insignificant. Sometimes they are simply uncomfortable explaining why they want to move.)

OFFICE STAFF

If you have rented commercial space for your business and have many students visiting your business every day (more than 20), you may want to hire a receptionist in addition to a booking person. Your receptionist should be warm and friendly, as well as patient with people from other countries. It can be difficult to understand students or their parents if they have heavy accents and minimal English-speaking skills.

ACTIVITIES STAFF

If activities are part of your business plan, you are best off having at least one person devoted to organizing and coordinating the "group fun." It goes without saying that activities people should be as outgoing and good at motivating activity in students as they are at organizing and multitasking. Also necessary are athletic ability, a keen understanding and appreciation of students' fears and desires, and knowledge of both indoor and outdoor activities available in the area.

Chapter 6

LOCATION AND FACILITIES

Tutorial services most often appeal to international students whose needs are not being met at the English institute they attend. The students are either lacking sufficient opportunity to practice their speaking skills in class (due to class size, excessive shyness caused by level imbalance among students, or ineffective teaching methods) or lacking the support needed to keep up with other students. Tutoring also appeals to affluent immigrants who want their children to succeed in public school and university. Regardless of who your customers are, your business should be in a location that is convenient for them.

If you choose to have an official site (e.g., an office), you will need to consider how easy it is for students to reach your location. In the case of adult international students, your business should be somewhere in the vicinity of other ESL-related organizations — private ESL institutes, for example, or even colleges or universities that have ESL programs. For the young-immigrant market, it is best for your business to be located in or near a safe neighborhood that contains high-income immigrant families.

If you do not plan to have an official site, but instead plan to have tutors and students meet elsewhere, the location of your business is less important. After all, your tutors will likely be traveling to the students' homes or to a public place that is easy for the student to get to. However, you still need a presentable space in which to hold information meetings and conduct evaluations. The space must be safe, centrally located, and easy for students and parents to reach. A quiet coffee shop or a table in a public library might be suitable.

Remember, businesses with an official tutoring site need the following:

- An office
- A consultation and/or testing room
- Tutoring rooms (each one large enough to accommodate a small group of students and a tutor)
- A computer room
- A lounge or eating area
- Restrooms (enough to accommodate your students and staff)

Businesses that do not have an official tutoring site need the following:

- A consultation and/or testing area
- Vehicle(s) with business insurance
- A number of possible tutoring locations

(If you are planning to use a particular coffee shop, library, or other public place for long periods of time, you might want to check with the management to make sure you have their permission. In the case of a coffee shop, you might even be able to strike a deal with the owner, in which you promise to purchase a certain amount of goods while you are there.)

Chapter 7

MARKETING

Effective marketing will ensure the success of your tutoring business. But what is the best way to market a service that is based as much on the right personality match (of student and tutor) as it is on teaching skills? In most cases, the magic formula is a combination of word-of-mouth advertising and professionally prepared marketing materials.

WORD-OF-MOUTH ADVERTISING

As with any type of personal-service industry, the best type of marketing for your tutorial service is word-of-mouth advertising. Once your business has earned a reputation for having reliable, results-oriented tutors, you won't need to spend money to spread the word about your services.

But how do you get the word out initially? Ideally, you would hire tutors who have a good reputation in the international-student community, or in your target immigrant community. Since students looking for one-on-one help prefer to hire tutors they know, or have heard about from their friends, linking up with well-established tutors will help you get your business off the ground quickly.

Why would an established tutor want or need to make connections with a new tutorial service? Some tutors who work from home would prefer to teach in a more spacious, more formal environment, equipped with business equipment and additional teaching materials. Tutors who have grown weary of the isolated work environment may seek out opportunities to expand their market and work with other like-minded people.

Another way to ensure that your tutors are reputable is to make connections with popular teachers from private ESL schools. Some teachers, given the option, would prefer the flexibility and choice that tutoring offers. Teachers who are well liked would likely bring with them a group of students who want to continue working with that particular teacher, even if it means changing learning venues.

If you don't have connections to reputable tutors or popular teachers, or if your staff is new to the area and therefore unknown to the local student population, the job of marketing your new business will be more difficult. Still, the only thing you need at the beginning is to get on the good side of a handful of students (or parents of students), who will tell their friends about what you and your team have to offer. In short, you and your team — including your marketer and tutors themselves — need to do some legwork by creating and distributing promotional materials to students, agents, industry representatives, and overseas organizations. When, where, and how you distribute your promotional materials will depend on the size and scope of your target market.

PROMOTIONAL MATERIAL

In addition to creating an attractive website, it is important to have professional-looking rack cards or brochures that can be distributed to places frequented by students, parents of students, agents, and industry representatives. Try to gain a presence in the following places:

- School bulletin boards

- Offices devoted to student services

- Child and youth organizations in high-end immigrant neighborhoods

- ESL and education-related trade fairs

- Public areas frequented by affluent non-native English speakers, such as specialty malls and stores

You might also want to try networking in less formal settings. Armed with some good-quality business cards that highlight your services and contact information, you could target pubs that attract the adult international-student community, or favorite parks and hangouts of foreign-born parents. Provided your conversation starts casually, with the intent of information gathering as opposed to "selling," you may be able to quickly spread a positive message about your services around your neighborhood.

A combination of professional marketing materials and effective networking techniques will help you land your first group of students. Making your marketing materials available to your first group of satisfied students will help spread the word to others. Many students participate in ESL chat rooms on the Internet, which are filled with comments about overseas experiences. Positive feedback about your staff will spread quickly and effortlessly.

AGENTS

Agents are people who have key connections to overseas institutions and student groups. Some agents live in overseas countries; others operate from the study country, in this case, the US or Canada. They act as the marketing liaison — students seek advice from them about which country to travel to and which school to attend; ESL schools strive to get on agents' lists of potential study destinations. Some agents also deal with tutors and tutoring businesses. Independent tutors and tutorial services can put up advertisements in agents' offices, or in communal areas visited by agency clients and in publications they read.

Building relationships with agents is a good idea for any new ESL business because most students prefer using agents over risking dealing directly with a "foreigner-run" school or tutoring business. Agents are likely to be familiar with study trends, and are therefore a valuable source of information when it comes to planning your programs.

Agents are often reluctant to work with newly established businesses. Those businesses that are welcomed into an agency pay for the privilege. Agents receive up to 50 percent commission from every student they place at a school or institution.

Because relationship building and maintenance is important in the ESL-marketing community, your marketing strategy should include ways to allow agents to hear about you from students themselves so that they'll want to do business with you in the future.

PROMOTIONS

A tutoring promotion is one way to attract students, especially during slow periods in your business. A promotion can be anything from a free lesson for every student referral to 50 percent off fees for the first month of tutoring if a student registers and pays for three months.

Since all students like to save money, the idea of a promotion that will boost student numbers makes sense. Indeed, it may be just the thing to turn the head of the international student who finds himself or herself short of next month's school tuition or the parent of a youngster approaching examination time. International students with upcoming departure dates also tend to cram some tutoring lessons into their schedules before heading home.

The danger in promotions — particularly over-the-top promotions that promise too much or seem too good to be true — is that they can be perceived by students and agents as "begging." After all, confident businesses rarely have promotions, presumably because they do not need help in attracting business. If you do choose to use promotions, exercise restraint. Plan the timing wisely, and make sure the type of promotion is suited to your target students. Keep in mind that in the long run, it is better for your business to be perceived as exclusive, or busy enough to have a waiting list, than so in need of students that you are willing to give your services away for free.

Chapter 8

POLICIES AND PROCEDURES

Making sure your tutorial service runs smoothly requires that you give some thought to operations-related rules and regulations. Having policies and procedures in place demonstrates to your customers that you are organized and experienced. It also helps ensure that problems, if and when they occur, are dealt with efficiently.

What kinds of problems should a tutorial service expect? There are many issues to consider. A student could dislike a tutor for an obscure or seemingly bizarre reason. (Some students are leery of people with reddish faces, as to them a red complexion is a sign of alcoholism.) There could also be problems with program changes and fee collection.

If your tutorial service has a formal location with a variety of programs, you might want to read through the Policies and Procedures section in Part 3 of this book for related issues. If you have a portable business, you will want to make sure that your new-student contract (see Sample 14 in Chapter 4) and orientation package address potential problems.

The process of collecting tutorial fees differs depending on the nature and style of your business. Formal operations offering a number of programs and employing several tutors may opt for a central payment system. That is, the business collects fees from the students and pays the tutors a wage.

Less formal businesses may simply refer prospective students to tutors, who are then responsible for keeping track of scheduling and collecting fees. The business would make money from both tutors and students through registration and administration or marketing fees, sales of education-related products and materials, and perhaps even tutorial-room rentals, if the business has this type of space available.

Regardless of your business setup, you need to have a solid payment system and a set of policies in place before you take on your first student. You need to make decisions about the following:

- *Registration fees:* Is a registration fee necessary? If so, how much is it?

- *Payment schedule:* Are students required to pay in advance? If so, how far in advance — one week, two weeks, one month, one program?

- *Late policy:* Does the clock start when a lesson is scheduled to begin, or when the student arrives? Or does it depend on how far in advance the tutor was informed of an altered start time?

- *Cancellation policy:* Are students required to pay for sessions they miss? If not, under what circumstances can they cancel a session without paying for it? How much notice must the student give when canceling a session?

- *Change policy:* Can students shorten, extend, or change their programs? If so, what is the procedure? Are there additional costs for changes?

Chapter **9**

MAINTAINING AND BUILDING YOUR CUSTOMER BASE

Imagine that your tutorial service is currently in operation and that you have a handful of students visiting your location on a regular basis. What can you do to ensure that they stay? How can you encourage them to tell their friends about the educational benefits they are receiving from you and your team?

The obvious answer is to treat your students as valuable customers, which means making sure you are delivering the high-quality programs and services they are paying for. But there is more you can do to ensure your customers are satisfied and eager to share their positive experiences with prospective customers. For example, you can learn from the experiences of other tutorial businesses and, anticipating potential problems, nip any problems in the bud before they bloom into something nasty and uncontrollable.

POTENTIAL PROBLEMS THAT COULD BECOME NASTY

Not all ESL tutors and tutorial services are created equal. Some students report having very bad experiences with tutors. For example, students have paid for lessons in advance but failed to receive the full number of tutoring hours that was agreed upon. Students have had to deal with perpetually late tutors who are rarely prepared, and seemingly disinterested and lackluster tutors who perk up only when an exchange of money is taking place. All of these situations can make students feel very uncomfortable and may cause them to look elsewhere for one-on-one help.

Some issues are mere misunderstandings resulting from cultural differences and a miscalculation of a student's needs, desires, and perceptions. For example, a student from a culture where age is tied to respect might not be comfortable with a tutor who is noticeably younger. Similarly, students from conservative cultures might not want to work with a tutor of the opposite sex. Another thing that might offend some students is poor attire. Students often find it difficult to take seriously a tutor dressed in tight or revealing clothing, as well as a tutor with an untidy appearance.

Below are some examples of things that tutoring service owners need to keep in check if they want to keep small problems small.

Wasting time

When screening your tutorial staff, be sure to find out their attitude toward time. To them, does "on time" mean ten minutes before the scheduled tutorial time? Fifteen minutes or five? What does "on time" mean to you?

Most students care about the time they devote to studying. Few are late, and those that are understand that they have to pay for the time they waste. However, even those who themselves are late have higher standards for their instructors. In other words, most students expect their tutor to be ready to work at the scheduled time, even if they themselves have fallen behind.

Tutors should do everything possible to avoid starting a lesson late. They should also end at the time they are scheduled to finish. Some students feel uncomfortable pointing to the clock, even if they have something they must do immediately after the lesson. To help keep lessons within the scheduled time, you can direct your tutors to stay in view of a clock, or keep a small clock or watch handy.

Failing to deliver the goods

Most students expect tutors to be organized and prepared for their lessons. Unfortunately, not all tutors show up to their tutorials ready to get down to business. What is more, some tutors do not see the harm in appearing a bit scatterbrained. While most students can accept the odd fumble, many lose respect for tutors who do not seem to be well organized. Tutors who always have to be reminded about where they left off at the end of the last lesson, or always forget information regarding a student's personal life — for example, how many siblings the student has — are sometimes perceived by the student as being unprepared and unprofessional. Even worse is the tutor who forgets to prepare or bring the handouts, materials, or resources promised during the last lesson.

You can help prevent your customers from thinking your tutors are unprofessional by being extra careful in your hiring practices. Part of finding good staff is offering decent enough wages to attract educators with high standards and a good work ethic. You can also help keep your tutors on track by creating a no-fail organizational system that allows them to go from student to student without getting confused about their roles or expectations on a given day. One simple way to do this is to give tutors a calendar-style overview of their tutorial sessions for an entire month, with each student represented by a different color (see Sample 16 in Chapter 4). The tutor can see at a glance which students require daily management and the most work, and which ones require a lighter commitment. By highlighting sessions after each one is complete, a tutor can quickly determine which students are committed to their program and which ones tend to skip or be late for class.

You can also give tutors a file on each student containing copies of the student's application form, evaluation form, and contract, as well as a lesson log that the tutor fills out at the end of each session, recording what was covered and what is planned for the next lesson (see Sample 15 in Chapter 4). A quick scan of these forms and records before a session is all a seasoned tutor needs to stay on track with a given student.

Another good thing about tutors with high standards and pay expectations is that they usually have more to offer in terms of ESL background. If you hire a TOEFL tutor, you will not have to worry about his or her knowledge of the more academic aspects of teaching ESL. A tutor who does not know how to explain key grammar points or give tips on reading comprehension will be little help to keen students trying to get into a North American university.

If even one of your tutors gains a reputation for incompetence, you could have a problem on your hands. Students who hear about that tutor through the grapevine might request that they not be given that tutor, causing awkwardness within your organization. Or an even worse situation could develop: your entire business could earn a poor reputation.

Too many changes and complications

One thing you want to be sure to avoid is putting students through many changes or scheduling complications over the course of their program. When possible, one student should work with one tutor (or team of tutors) in one location at one set time. The more cancellations, changes, and substitute teaching that occurs — due to holidays, illness, or appointments — and the more shuffling around of

tutoring times and places, the less students will take your business seriously.

In fact, some students may even try to take advantage of the situation. They might, for example, try to persuade you to give them a special deal on account of the inconveniences they have suffered. Or they might use the situation to justify a previously planned move to another institution. Further complications around their departure could lead to other students losing faith in your programs, and in your business in general.

For the most part, change is disturbing to students, particularly those who come from countries where the education system is designed to maintain sameness and consistency. Students often have the same teacher for a number of classes throughout the school year. They study with the same classmates too, and consequently build solid relationships with them. In North America, by contrast, change is neither unusual nor seen as negative in terms of its impact on a student's learning.

Inappropriate attire

Students from conservative countries sometimes feel uncomfortable with how North Americans dress for work. Accustomed to teachers and tutors who wear formal or dressy clothing, some students have a difficult time with casual dress at work. People in the ESL industry particularly tend to dress down. It is not uncommon for tutors meeting with students in coffee shops to wear ragged or torn jeans and a rumpled shirt. Even worse is the female tutor who wears a low-cut blouse and tight, low-rise pants. While appropriate for an evening out, this type of clothing can cause problems for you and your business, as students invariably view such clothing as unprofessional.

Most students will be too shy to admit that poor clothing choices bother them, so your business may lose students without your knowing exactly why.

To prevent problems before they start, you may want to include a dress code in a tutor policy manual or employee manual if you choose to create one. If not, be sure to discuss the matter fully when interviewing tutors for permanent or contract positions.

LITTLE THINGS THAT PROMOTE TEAM SPIRIT IN YOUR STUDENTS

Ideally, your tutoring business will blossom into a place that encourages both language learning and camaraderie in its students and staff. Whether you have a formal location — with an office, tutorial rooms, and a common area — or conduct most of your business over the telephone or Internet, you will want to create an atmosphere that draws in new students.

So, how do you build team spirit among students who are taught individually and at different times during the week? There are several ways to make your students feel part of something important and worth telling their friends about.

Newsletters

Creating a newsletter is one way of creating a feeling of belonging and cohesiveness in your students and staff. It also serves as a vehicle for conveying information. Whether in print form or part of your website, your newsletter could feature brief biographies and photos of successful pupils, information about upcoming academic and social events, study tips, and news about your business or community. You could even publish samples of students' prose or poetry, or help those hoping for a career in print media get started by "hiring" them to do regular interviews and stories for the newsletter.

Contests

Another way to keep students connected is to hold contests that draw students together in a common pursuit. A spelling bee, a short-story-writing contest, and even a timed TOEFL essay-writing contest are examples of competitions that bring students together. Another fun challenge for students is participation in word games such as Scrabble, or general-knowledge games such as modified versions of *Jeopardy!* and *Who Wants to Be a Millionaire*.

Your contests need not be related to academic subjects or even the acquisition of English. In fact, you could hold contests related to almost anything that interests your students — a video-game challenge, a pie-eating contest, or a competition related to art or music.

Prizes may encourage your students to participate. The grand-prize winner could receive a discount on tuition, while other winners could receive smaller prizes — a dictionary or thesaurus, movie tickets, or a CD or DVD.

Get-togethers and outings

In the same way that light competition can unite students who do not have an opportunity to study together, get-togethers encourage a sense of camaraderie and belonging. Of course, there are obvious occasions and times of year to hold a party — Valentine's Day, Easter, Halloween, Christmas — but you can also create your own celebrations and themes.

You could create a new ESL-related holiday such as Grammar Day or Vocabulary-building Day.

Routine outings are also helpful in building community spirit. You could, for example, have weekend Walk 'n' Talk sessions on a local hiking trail. Students of all ages, levels, and backgrounds could get some exercise and practice their English-speaking skills in a low-pressure, nonclassroom setting.

A picnic, movie night, or bowling event — the list of options is endless. The key is to understand your target market well enough to know what kinds of get-togethers and outings they see as fun, worth attending, and worth spreading the word about.

One thing you can rely on is that almost any kind of get-together or outing that includes interaction with native English speakers will attract ESL students. For example, if your market is adult international students, you could host a back-to-school party or a cross-cultural-exchange event and invite a group of English-speaking university students to join the festivities. Being given the opportunity to communicate with English speakers of similar age and experience is a big bonus for international students, and one they are very likely to tell their friends about.

Enticing university students to socialize with international students might require incentives such as free food or the opportunity to see or do something interesting (watch music videos from other countries, make a traditional food or craft, etc.). Another way to attract university students is to demonstrate how participation in the event could be added to their résumé and applications for programs requiring keen communication skills and heightened cultural awareness. Students who want to become teachers could benefit in many ways from befriending people from the international-student community.

Being open to extras

A surefire way to earn the trust and respect of students is to show them that their voices are heard. When students know that their concerns are taken seriously, and that their suggestions of ways to make your business more attractive and comfortable are valued and carefully weighed, most will be satisfied and less likely to criticize weaknesses in your operation.

By listening carefully to the comments and requests of your students on an ongoing basis, you will have an advantage over other education-related facilities: you will know precisely what you need to do to maintain and attract more business. And because the tutoring business is by nature a flexible, individually defined, open-ended form of education, there is plenty of opportunity for change and reconsideration of services.

For example, suppose you have a formal location that is somewhat difficult for students to get to by bus. If you know that students are struggling with transportation, you can arrange an alternative — a pickup system or a car-pool arrangement. You could even invent a solution: you could hire native English-speaking companions to take students to their lessons.

If your tutors are working with school-age kids at their homes after school, you might offer their parents a few extras to ensure timely starts and full use of the lesson time, such as picking up the student from school and giving him or her a healthy snack or drink to boost energy.

Taking initiative and showing that you are willing to consider anything that might make tutoring easier and more successful will ultimately pay off. Students know when they are being well taken care of, and they will show their appreciation by registering for more lessons and introducing other students to your business.

If you think starting and running a tutorial service is a good fit for you, take a look at Part 4 to find out more about the practical aspects of running a business. Then complete Checklist 2 to make sure you have considered all the details before launching your new venture.

CHECKLIST 2
OPENING AN ESL TUTORIAL SERVICE

Before you open the doors to your ESL tutorial service, make sure you have considered the following:

❑ Do you have a thorough understanding of the "students as customers" concept?

❑ Have you researched current industry information and gained an understanding of current trends?

❑ Do you have a clearly defined target market that you understand well?

❑ Have you developed a "big picture" plan of your core services?

❑ Do you have a clearly defined "snapshot" of a typical contract (from consulting session to final session)?

❑ Have you developed a monitoring system linking the initial evaluation (consulting session) to the final evaluation?

❑ If you are working with a team, have you hired key staff?

❑ Have you made contact with others whose services you may require?

❑ Have you gathered the necessary office and administration forms?

❑ Do you have an accessible location and adequate facilities?

❑ Have you created a website and marketing materials?

PART 2 EXERCISES

Exercise 2

Researching Tutorial Services in Your Area

Do some research into tutorial services in and around your area. Record your findings on student profiles, expectations, and fees.

Exercise 3

Determining What Kind of Tutorial Service Works for You

Determine which tutorial services are missing and needed in your area. Next, make a list of any new or untapped markets on the horizon. Identify the ones that are of most interest to you.

Exercise 4

Drafting a Student Profile for Your Tutoring Business

Drawing on your notes from Exercises 2 and 3, draft a detailed student profile for your tutoring business.

Exercise 5

Drafting a Mission Statement for Your Tutorial Service

Clarify the purpose of the services you provide by drafting a mission statement for your tutorial service.

Exercise 6

Drafting a Methodology Description for Your Tutorial Service

Draft an outline of how your tutorial service will deliver its services.

Exercise 7

Drafting a Marketing Promise for Your Tutorial Service

Create a list of characteristics that make your school competitive and demonstrate your understanding of your target market.

Exercise 8

Drafting an Entrance and Exit Assessment System

Outline your tutorial service's system of evaluation.

Exercise 9

Drafting a Programs and Services Schedule for Your Tutorial Service

Consider the programs you plan to offer and think about the resources and learning materials you will need. Use this information to define your tutoring methods, and draft a detailed list of your programs and services.

Exercise 10
Drafting a Tutor Schedule

Use the table below to map out a tutor schedule. Create a coding system that reflects your business's policies and mandate.

Tutor name:_____ Program(s):_____

	Monday	Tuesday	Wednesday	Thursday	Friday	Saturday	Sunday	Total Hours
Week 1								
Week 2								
Week 3								
Week 4								

Locations:

Status:

Students:

Exercise 11
Determining Key Roles and Responsibilities in Your Tutorial Service

Consider the key staff members you plan to employ as part of your tutorial service. Will you or anyone else on your team be required to take on multiple roles? Make a list of the roles and key responsibilities of each staff member.

Exercise 12
Describing Your Location and Facilities

What kind of tutoring business do you plan to have? Provide a detailed description of your location and facilities.

Exercise 13
Drafting a Marketing Plan for Your Tutorial Service

Describe in detail how you plan to market your services both prior to opening your tutoring business and while in business.

Exercise 14
Drafting a System for Collecting Fees for Your Tutorial Service

Refer to Chapter 8 and then outline your system for collecting student fees.

Exercise 15
Drafting an Orientation Package for Your Students

Consider the issues that may arise in your business. Make a list of the policies and procedures you plan to include in your new-student orientation package.

Exercise 16
Maintaining and Building Your Customer Base

What are your plans for maintaining and building your customer base? Make a list of things you would consider offering or doing for your students.

Part 3

STARTING AND RUNNING AN ESL SCHOOL

Chapter 10

EXPLORING YOUR MARKET

So you've decided to run a school, rather than a tutorial service. What comes next? Your first step is to figure out exactly what kind of school you want to run. To do this, you need to define your target market and decide what kind of programs you will offer. You also need to think about what will set your school apart from other schools, thereby attracting the kind of students you are targeting. Is it your location? Is it your team's reputation for being experts in a particular area of study? Or is it something about your classroom demographics, such as extra-small class size or an impressive mix of countries represented in each class? Perhaps it is a combination of these things.

In this part of the book, you will be given information and tips on how to define your market. Once you have completed the exercises, you will be well on your way to developing your school's business plan (see Part 4).

CLARIFYING YOUR MARKET

To determine your target market, you need to understand current ESL industry trends:

- How many international students come to your country each year?

- Which countries are best represented in the international-student population?

- What are the most popular cities in which to study, and why?

- What kinds of programs are students currently enrolled in, and why?

- How much do they usually pay for English classes?

To find answers to these questions, start by visiting government websites that have immigration statistics, or visit your local library and ask a librarian to assist you. You can also find information on the web by doing a search for the terms "international schools" and "international students," and spending a bit of time browsing, reading, and collecting information.

If you are interested in working with the immigrant population, similar questions arise:

- How many non-English-speaking immigrants arrive in your country each year?
- Where do they usually settle, and why?
- What kinds of English programs are currently available to them?
- How much, if anything, do the programs cost?
- Do adult immigrants have children who require extra help with learning English?

By visiting immigration-related websites or talking to your local librarian, you will find answers to many of these questions. For information on English classes available to immigrants, contact immigrant-services agencies in your area.

DETERMINING YOUR TARGET MARKET

Now that you have a clear sense of current industry realities, you can use the information you have gathered to create an image of the typical classroom you expect to see in your future school. Look around your imaginary classroom and ask yourself the following:

- Where are my students from? Are they from Asia, South America, Europe, or a mix of places?
- How old are my students? Are they teenagers, university age, adults, a mix of ages, or are they children?
- Are my students newcomers to North America, or have they been here for a while and now looking for alternatives to their current study situations? Or is there a mix of both types?
- Are my students academically oriented youth who are planning to take the TOEFL or TOEIC? Are they young people looking for a fun overseas experience? Are they business-internship students or working-holiday-visa students who hope to gain overseas work experience? Are they immigrants who need help with daily life in a new country?

CONSIDERING WHICH PROGRAMS BEST MATCH YOUR MARKET

With a clear picture in your head of a typical classroom scenario, you can begin organizing programs that match your students' needs, desires, and most importantly, perceptions.

Some of your program planning will be obvious. For example, a school that targets young-adult students with academic goals needs to offer English programs that aim to enhance students' academic performance. A school that offers test preparation courses, such as TOEFL and TOEIC, will be more attractive to this group of students than an outdoor adventure ESL school or a conversation club.

By contrast, a school that targets students looking for overseas adventure and an exciting cultural experience should focus on courses that help students communicate better with local people. Conversation-based programs will be more attractive to this group of students than courses in essay writing or other types of academic preparation.

Many schools offer a range of programs, hoping to attract a variety of students. While larger operations can do this with ease because of space, resources, and sheer numbers of students, smaller schools are better off developing a reputation for strongly delivering a smaller number of specialized programs than trying to be everything to every type of student.

Knowing your target market and offering courses that your students understand to be of value will ensure student satisfaction. And with student satisfaction comes word-of-mouth advertising and increased status within the ESL industry.

MAKING YOUR MARK

To aid in the building of a reputable institution, you need to find a niche that sets you apart from your competitors. Some schools, for example, have a distinctive location. A recent trend in the industry is for students to study in small, friendly communities where most of the residents speak English. Unlike large cities, which house people with various ethnic backgrounds and languages, the English-only small-town environment forces students to use daily what they have learned inside the classroom.

Some small-town school owners have taken the "safe and friendly" aspect of small towns to the extreme by transforming large homes — on the beach or in the countryside — into alternative learning environments. These settings are attractive to students who have grown weary of the stiffer, more traditional "concrete" institutions located in cities. Studying in a home-like environment makes some students feel more comfortable in their struggle to master a new language. Adding beautiful surroundings to the mix only makes students' overseas experiences that much more memorable.

Another way for a school to stand out is to develop a reputation for offering unique programs that guarantee success. Some schools, for example, have a reputation for offering highly effective listening programs. Students who are weak in listening skills but require a certain skill level for a specific purpose — taking the TOEFL or TOEIC, for example — flock to these schools to ensure they get the practice they need. Some schools with specialized programs have long waiting lists.

Other ways to make a name for your school have to do with classroom demographics. Small class size is important to most language learners. A school that boasts a maximum class size of 6 or 8 students will be more attractive than one with a 14-student limit. Student quotas that limit the number of students of any one nationality in a particular class can also be appealing. Many students dislike being in classes where most of the other students come from the same country as they do. For some students, the opportunity to mix and build relationships with people of other cultures and nationalities is an important factor in their decision to study abroad.

RESPONDING TO YOUR MARKET

Now that you have decided basic things about your school — target market, types of programs you might offer, ideas regarding your competitive edge — your next step is to thoroughly investigate the needs, desires, and perceptions of your target market, and decide whether or not you are prepared to respond to them.

In many ways, your students are your customers. They are paying for your products and services, and if they are unhappy with what they get, they will find satisfaction somewhere else. Most international students have set ideas about what they need to learn, as well as how classes should be delivered and how teachers and students should conduct themselves. It is important to understand your students' prior experiences so that you can understand their reactions to your school's structure and teaching methods.

Understanding your students as customers will help you make better business decisions, and responding positively to their requests and expectations will guarantee that you will make money. By contrast, making unsubstantiated assumptions about your students can cost you dearly.

Student needs

Some school owners and teachers reject the "students as customers" model and make the mistake of assuming they understand their students' needs better than the students

themselves. This can be true especially of people who have education degrees and experience teaching in public schools. Often, they feel they must "educate" students, rather than simply help them with language development. In other words, some teachers want to teach their students *how* and *what* to think, rather than how to express their beliefs — whatever they may be — in English.

Some teachers mistakenly think their role is to teach students how to think differently, which all too often means "how to think like a Westerner." Students who feel pressured to accept, and even adopt, cultural beliefs that are different from their own will not stay in a school for very long. While they usually enjoy learning about what other people believe, students understandably become uncomfortable when a teacher suggests that their cultural beliefs are false or inferior.

Student desires

On a similar note, some schools make the mistake of assuming that their students' desires are the same as their own. For example, they believe their hardworking students want to relax and have fun while overseas (because that is what the school owners and teachers would want if they were studying abroad), when in fact the students prefer to focus on learning and language acquisition. Some students invest their savings (or their parents' savings) in their tuition and living expenses. Many feel pressure to learn a great deal of English in a very short time. Having fun may not interest them, unless they can see that fun will enhance their skills. Schools that over-encourage students to relax and have a good time may upset students and make them feel they have wasted their money.

Some schools have spent small fortunes marketing aspects of their facilities that do not interest their students in the least. On the Sunshine Coast of British Columbia, for example, one start-up school was convinced that international students from busy Asian cities would jump at the chance to study in a quiet, seaside town, with a wide variety of outdoor activities and ample opportunity to enjoy nature. While most of the students appreciated the beauty of their surroundings, they were not particularly interested in outdoor recreation. They reluctantly participated in the outdoor activities that were offered — hiking, camping, canoeing — all the while longing for activities that were familiar to them, such as shopping, singing at a karaoke bar, and socializing with friends at pubs and nightclubs. The school owners soon realized they had made false assumptions about their students' desires. As a result, the owners had to resist basing the activities they offered on what they themselves thought were worth doing, and instead communicate more effectively with students about their extracurricular interests.

Student perceptions

One of the most difficult tasks for any ESL-school owner is dealing with students' perceptions of the facility, programs, and staff.

As in any business, perception is as important as reality. If customers feel they are not getting value for their money, they will complain. And if they receive unsatisfactory service, they will complain. Because your students are paying customers, they have a right to insist that what they are buying meets certain standards.

Problems can arise when students' standards and values are not in line with their schools' standards and values. For example, many Asian students have expectations about the way teachers should dress and conduct classes. They may be used to formal attire and a formal teaching approach. If they enroll in an ESL school that allows teachers to dress casually and promotes informal teaching methods, students may perceive the school and staff as unprofessional. Regardless of which approach actually works better in terms of learning a language, students' perception of what works and what doesn't will influence both their comfort level and acceptance of their surroundings.

Some school owners insist that students need to understand and accept Western teaching practices in order to learn English, and many work hard to change students' perceptions of ESL education and the North American way of doing things. Battling perceptions can be exhausting as well as costly.

The importance of perception goes well beyond the classroom. Your marketing materials will come under scrutiny from customers as well. A school with a well-developed website and high-quality promotional materials will attract more attention than a school with amateur web graphics and poorly made brochures.

Marketing is costly, so it is important to consider what your students will perceive when faced with your material. One large ESL school learned this lesson of perception the hard way when they discovered that the free gifts they were giving to new students were immediately being discarded. The school had invested money in backpacks and T-shirts displaying the school's logo. Every new student received a backpack and T-shirt with his or her orientation package. What the school did not realize was that their market — primarily Korean young adults — prefers to wear brand-name clothing and accessories. Many of the backpacks and shirts ended up in dumpsters. If the school owner had known how school logos were perceived by his market, he could have saved the school thousands of dollars.

So, how exactly do you turn your market research into a dynamite ESL school? You need to learn to take information and create a niche for yourself.

According to a series of articles published in the *Vancouver Sun* in October 2004, these were the most common complaints among international students attending Vancouver-area schools:

1. Homesickness

2. Failure to meet North American friends

3. Lack of English improvement

Knowing what students are *not* happy about provides you with an opportunity to create a school that fulfills a clearly defined need. But first you must understand the origins of the problem.

The complaints listed above are interrelated. Homesickness is a normal reaction to any kind of move away from what is familiar. But it is particularly painful when people are halfway around the world from family, friends, and possibly a significant other. Students hope to override their feelings of loneliness by making new friends, preferably ones who are native English speakers. Making friends with English speakers provides students with social contact and the opportunity to practice and improve their English in a low-stress, noncompetitive environment.

Unfortunately, few students have the confidence or courage to go out and make North American friends, and therefore most students find little opportunity to speak English outside of class. As a result, students often feel isolated and look for solace in people whom they understand and trust — people who speak the same language. However, making friends with people from the same country can make students feel guilty. They may even question their decision to study abroad in the first place. They may ask themselves, "Why did I spend all this money to study overseas when I'm not using my English skills? Should I have just stayed in my country and gone to a private English school?"

The more students stick together or socialize in large groups, the less likely they are to improve their English. This is because they are not putting into practice what they have learned in class, and to others, they appear to be a group of tourists. English-speaking North Americans are unlikely to approach a group of people who are speaking another language and try to befriend them. Friendships develop when people discover things they have in common and begin to build on them.

So how can this circular problem become the foundation for a language school? You could create programs that focus on helping students make the most of their free time. The programs could be geared to teaching students the practical language and social skills necessary to make friends with native English speakers. Students could learn anything from cultural norms in social situations to commonly used expressions. The classes could be designed to help students overcome shyness and other barriers to effective networking and socializing, such as pronunciation and intonation difficulties.

By finding ways to tackle the issues most troubling to students, entrepreneurial school owners have the opportunity to build a reputation for themselves in a niche market. And by understanding students as customers, school owners are more likely to keep abreast of market influences and trends in the ESL industry, thereby ensuring that students are satisfied with what they have purchased.

Chapter  **11**

YOUR SCHOOL, YOUR PROGRAMS

Your programs are the "meat and potatoes" of your school. They define who you are to the outside world, and they are key to the success of your institution.

More than anything, your programs are of primary concern to your students. Therefore, you need to make careful decisions about what you offer and how your courses are delivered. Your programs need to be structured enough to demonstrate a sense of order, but flexible enough to allow for modification when necessary. You also need to market your programs in language that your students, or "customers," understand. That is, you need to appeal to the sensibilities of your market.

Some schools begin to offer classes before clearly mapping out and defining their programs, believing they will be able to pull things together later on when the business is up and running smoothly and, presumably, there is time to consider such things. This approach, however, invariably leads to more work and more headaches than necessary. There is rarely time for such luxuries when your business is fully operational. It is much easier and more efficient to develop a big-picture plan and use it for program development *before* welcoming students into the classroom. What is more, your efforts in the first few months should be geared toward fine-tuning and improving your big-picture plan and programs, rather than creating them.

BIG-PICTURE PLANNING

Having a clear sense of the big picture will help you manage and "sell" your school programs effectively. As a school owner, it is important to be able to describe and discuss in detail how your programs and evaluation system fit together.

In mapping out your programs, you need to do the following:

- Create a student profile.
- Define your mission statement.
- Clarify your delivery method.
- Define your market niche.
- Develop a program overview.
- Create an evaluation system that ties everything together.

Creating a student profile

The kinds of programs you offer will depend on the kinds of students in your area. Therefore, the first step in program development is having a clear picture of your target market. Based on your market research and understanding of current industry trends and issues, you need to create a detailed profile of your typical student.

Sample 17 provides an example of a student profile.

Determining the purpose of your programs (mission statement)

A key part of big-picture planning involves clarifying your school's purpose. What do you hope to accomplish in terms of your students' progress? What do you hope your students will be able to do upon leaving your school? What sets your programs apart from those offered at other institutions? What is your mission statement?

For example, you might decide to focus on helping students improve their spoken English. And knowing that the goal of many students is to make North American friends, you could choose to specialize in classes that teach students to speak with the intonation and speed of a native English speaker.

SAMPLE 17
PROFILE OF STUDENTS

Profile of ABC Institute's Students

- In early to mid-20s
- From Asia
- University students
- Need overseas English experience on résumé to get a good job after graduating from university
- First time away from home
- Plan to study overseas for six months
- Want to make North American friends
- Hope to see rapid improvement in oral English ability

The mission statement in Sample 18 reflects the above goal.

Clarifying your delivery method

Next, you need to clarify how you are going to ensure that your mission statement rings true. What do your teachers need to understand about the school's mission in order to prepare lessons? How are they going to put into practice your philosophy of ESL education?

For example, if your school aims to help students speak with the speed and accuracy of a native English speaker, at all times your teachers must keep in mind the focus on oral communication. They should also use methods that emphasize the importance of intonation, linking of sounds, and pronunciation of individual words. Finally, your teachers should provide students with the opportunity to learn language that is both practical and relevant to their current situation and future goals.

In a case such as this, your school's "methodology statement" might look something like Sample 19.

Defining the ways in which your school fills a market niche

In Chapter 10, you were asked to think of things that make your school unique. Now you need to articulate the ways in which your programs fill a market niche.

For example, knowing that students often get into a vicious circle — their homesickness leads to depression and a lack of confidence, both of which hinder their ability to make

SAMPLE 18
MISSION STATEMENT

ABC Institute Mission Statement

At ABC Institute, our mission is to help international students speak with confidence and

accuracy — at native-speaker speed — about matters that are relevant and important to them.

SAMPLE 19
METHODOLOGY STATEMENT

ABC Institute Methodology Statement

- ABC Institute aims to help students develop the speaking skills necessary to both communicate with native English speakers and pursue their English-related academic and/or career goals.

- Our programs focus on communication rather than content. We help with the practical application of grammar rather than the absorption of ideas, facts, or issues.

- Our methods involve identifying, perfecting, and building on what students already know.

English-speaking friends — your school could offer educational remedies and emphasize its commitment to results. Your marketing materials should highlight your school's unique qualities. See Sample 20.

Developing a program overview

Your next order of business involves the practical application of theory and philosophy. In other words, you need to develop a program overview that outlines all the courses you offer. The overview should be easy to read and include information about term length, program length, study times, and student levels.

Typically, a term lasts four weeks, and a program consists of three terms (12 weeks). This may be because many textbooks feature 12 chapters.

Most schools offer a minimum of three levels: beginner, intermediate, and advanced. Levels are often determined by grammar level and fluency. There are many well-established systems of determining language level. Most textbook series are similarly divided into categories based on grammar level. You may want to use the textbook series you have chosen as your guide to determining language level. You could also develop your own system.

Large schools with high student numbers sometimes further differentiate within traditional levels by using the terms "upper" and "lower," as in "upper beginner" and "lower beginner." Because some students are sensitive about being classified as a beginner, particularly after having studied English for a significant period of time, some schools have used euphemisms such as "pre-intermediate" to identify lower levels. Other schools have tried to avoid labeling altogether and instead use colors or symbols to distinguish levels, thus avoiding the word "beginner" and keeping competition among intermediate and advanced students to a minimum.

Common among many schools is the idea of core programs being offered in the morning and electives in the afternoon. Your school's core program needs to be particularly reflective of your core group of students. For example, if your market is university-bound students, you may want to offer Academic English classes in the mornings.

Generally speaking, your electives can be more flexible in terms of program length, and more varied with regard to content. For instance, you might offer a two-term business program or a one-term course on pronunciation and intonation. Students who are happy

SAMPLE 20
MARKETING PROMISE

ABC Marketing Institute Marketing Promise

At ABC Institute, we guarantee the following:

- Small, student-centered classes (a maximum of six students)
- Emphasis on increasing speed and accuracy, with at least 50 percent of each class devoted to speaking development and practice
- Our commitment to understanding and responding to students' practical needs and future goals

---

with their core classes will be more willing to try new things in the afternoon, even if the classes are not entirely of interest to them.

When developing an overview of your school's programs, ensure that each course is clearly coded. Taking the time to do a thorough job of organizing and labeling programs and classes when you are starting your business will help you stay focused and save you the headache of trying to sort out a mess of levels, term numbers, and class names later on.

For example, supposing your target market is most interested in developing their communication skills (rather than academic skills), you could create a morning program that stresses function over vocabulary building and academic testing. Your morning program overview could look similar to Sample 21.

The afternoon electives could be a mix of functional and academic classes. Students could be given a list of options before the start of a new term, and the most popular picks would be offered that term. Electives can be one-month specialty courses or multi-month programs.

Your afternoon program choices could look something like Sample 22, and a typical term might look something like Sample 23.

Establishing a system of evaluation

With your big-picture program plan complete, your next task is to create a system of evaluation that will regulate the movement of students into, through, and out of classes.

To do this, you first need to create a method of assessing incoming students' levels. You also need to create a term assessment or a way in which teachers can measure students' progress. This could take the form of tests and quizzes, presentations and projects, or a combination of these. Of course, certain forms of evaluation are better suited to certain types of classes. For example, testing is better for TOEFL classes, while presentations are better for public-speaking classes. Term assessments help teachers decide whether a student should move up a level.

Another form of term assessment may be required in cases where a student challenges the teacher's perception of his or her abilities.

SAMPLE 21
MORNING PROGRAM OVERVIEW

ABC Institute Morning Program Overview

English Communication Program (ECP): Monday to Friday, 9:00 a.m. to 12:00 p.m.

Level	Term 1	Term 2	Term 3
Beginner	ECP B1	ECP B2	ECP B3
Intermediate	ECP I1	ECP I2	ECP I3
Advanced	ECP A1	ECP A2	ECP A3

AFTERNOON PROGRAM CHOICES

ABC Institute Electives Program Overview

Beginner

- Conversation (3 terms: Con. b1, Con. b2, Con. b3)
- Pronunciation (2 terms: Pro. b1, Pro. b2)
- Idioms and Slang (2 terms: Idioms b1, Idioms b2)
- Paragraph Writing (1 term: Writing b)

Intermediate

- Conversation (3 terms: Con. i1, Con. i2, Con. i3)
- Reading and Literature (2 terms: Reading i1, Reading i2)
- Current Events (2 terms: Cur. Events i1, Cur. Events i2)
- TOEFL (2 terms: TOEFL i1, TOEFL i2)
- TOEIC (2 terms: TOEIC i1, TOEIC i2)
- Business Writing (1 term: Bus. Writing i)

Advanced

- TOEFL (2 terms: TOEFL a1, TOEFL a2)
- TOEIC (2 terms: TOEIC a1, TOEIC a2)
- Business Writing (2 terms: Bus. a1, Bus. a2)
- Public Speaking (2 terms: Pub. Speaking a1, Pub. Speaking a2)

Students may feel their level of English is higher (or lower) than it really is. They may not agree with their teacher's evaluation and may want to be measured in a different way. In a case such as this, a level test endorsed by the school can be used.

Lastly, you need a departing-student assessment that can be cross-checked against a student's initial assessment. This allows the student to see how much he or she has learned while attending your school. It also serves as a marketing tool for prospective students: when your marketing materials give an example of a student whose English has improved dramatically as a result of your programs, they may be more inclined to study at your institution.

Your evaluation system should be independent of the course evaluations used by teachers in the classroom, yet not inconsistent with them. First, you need to establish the abilities of a beginner-level student. What grammar terms are they able and unable to use? What about fluency? Listening ability? Pronunciation? The same goes for intermediate- and advanced-level students.

SAMPLE 23
AFTERNOON PROGRAM OVERVIEW

ABC Institute Electives Schedule

Monday to Thursday

Time	Elective
1:00–1:55	Pronunciation b1
2:05–3:00	Idioms and Slang b1
1:00–1:55	Current Events i1
2:05–3:00	TOEFL i1
1:00–1:55	Business Writing a1
2:05–3:00	TOEIC a1

The easiest way in which to do this is to use the measurements used in the textbook series you have chosen. Some schools try to merge an independent evaluation system with the system used in their textbooks. While this is certainly a valid approach, merging two disparate systems can mean a great deal of work.

Sample 24 describes one system of evaluation.

PROGRAM DEVELOPMENT

Program development refers to the act of breathing life into your big-picture program plans. That is, filling in the details — deciding which textbooks and/or materials to use, and working out a system that can easily be explained to new teachers who come on board. Your system should also be easy enough that it can be explained to new students both in person and in your marketing materials.

Developing a course outline

Whether you opt for textbooks or choose to create your own materials, you should clearly define and map out which chapters or themes will be covered in a given term, and over the course of each program.

It is also a good idea to draft course outlines for each term, highlighting such things as the objective of the course, the materials that will be used, and the system by which students will be evaluated. Course outlines should be given to students on the first day of a new term. Doing this helps students understand what to expect, as well as what is expected of them. Course outlines also show that your classes and teachers are well organized. Students usually like to see evidence of order and organization. They want to know they are not wasting their time and money at a school that is making things up as it goes along. Start-up schools must be especially

SAMPLE 24
EVALUATION SYSTEM

Suppose you have decided to use videotaped interviews as your incoming-student assessment and departing-student assessment tool. And suppose you have decided to use the *Fundamentals of English Grammar* series — beginner, intermediate, and advanced — for your core program. Your system of evaluation might look something like this.

ABC Institute Evaluation System

Incoming-Student Assessment

Strategy:

- Videotaped response to: "Tell me about yourself."
- Written response to: "Describe, in detail, your trip from your home country to the city you live in now."

Terms of assessment:

- Assessor listens/reads for vocabulary level, grammar usage, and fluency.
- Student is assessed based on *Fundamentals'* grammar model, and then placed in the appropriate class.

Term Assessment/Level-to-Level Assessment

Strategy:

- Student is tested regularly throughout the term.
- A term assessment (oral plus other) is given on the second-to-last day of the term.

Terms of assessment:

- The teacher decides if the student should move laterally or vertically.

Departing-Student Assessment

Strategy:

- Videotaped response to: "Tell me about yourself."
- Written response to: "Describe, in detail, your experience of living in the US."

Terms of assessment:

- Assessor listens/reads for vocabulary level, grammar usage, and fluency.
- Student is shown the differences between his or her incoming-student assessment and departing-student assessment.

---

careful about making a good impression on students. Solid planning and organization are key to early success.

Sample 25 is an example of a course outline for an academic class, while Sample 26 is an example of a student evaluation form.

Using a textbook series

If you are using textbooks, try to find a series that matches your target market's language needs. For example, nonacademic students usually prefer light, practical content that is soft on grammar explanations and exercises, while academic students need textbooks that offer heavier reading components and thorough grammar and vocabulary exercises. The best textbooks are the ones that encourage a great deal of paired and small-group conversation in the classroom, but also include homework exercises — or even a separate workbook — requiring students to read and write at their own speed during their own time.

With a textbook series, program development might be as easy as deciding to cover one or two units per week, with supplementary material brought in to add variety and enhance lessons. The system of evaluation might be testing vocabulary retention at the end of the week, and having students do presentations or projects on textbook-related themes at the end of the term.

Using a textbook series is certainly easier and faster than creating your own materials from scratch. The right set of books can save you a great deal of time and money, since they do the topic and grammar organization for you. However, there are disadvantages to using textbooks. For one, they are expensive. If you choose a series that turns out to be ill suited to your students, you could end up wasting a substantial amount of money. You also run the risk of using the same book as competing schools. Students who transfer to your school will not be happy to find they are repeating a topic or unit they did the week before at another school. This situation can throw a wrench into a well-prepared teacher's monthly plan and usually results in the teacher having to find an alternative at the last minute.

You can save money by using class sets of textbooks. This means that the books stay in the classroom and are used during class time only. The problem with this system is that some students resent not being able to write in the books and not being able to take them home for review. Lending out books overnight is possible, but invariably problems arise in keeping track of individual copies. Students sometimes steal books or accidentally keep them when they leave a school. Photocopying textbook units or exercises is possible in some cases, but there are usually copyright issues to contend with.

Lastly, a duplication problem arises when a particular textbook is used for more than one class or level. A grammar book, for example, might be used in a grammar class, a TOEFL class, and even a conversation class (in cases where supplementary materials are needed to clarify a troubling grammar point used in conversation).

Creating your own programs

If you decide not to use a textbook series as a base, you will have to come up with an alternative system that is easy for both teachers and students to understand. For example, suppose you want to use the English Communication Program introduced earlier as your core morning program. Because the program is function based, with a focus on oral communication, you may want to develop your own system and materials, such as in the example given in Sample 27.

Thinking about program themes

It is usually best if the teacher and students choose a program theme at the start of the term. The theme should be broad enough to allow for flexibility within and between levels. That is, a beginner class with a food theme will be completely different in terms of vocabulary, grammar, and presentation expectations than an intermediate or advanced class on the same theme. A beginner class might learn to give instructions on how to make a meal, while an intermediate class might learn dinner-conversation techniques. An advanced class might discuss genetically modified foods or mad cow disease.

The following themes are broad enough for use with any level of students:

- Art
- Education
- Environment
- Food
- Health
- Home
- Media
- Music
- Relationships
- Science
- Travel
- Work

To see how one theme can be used for multiple levels, take a look at Sample 28.

COURSE OUTLINE FOR AN ACADEMIC CLASS

Academic English — Lower Intermediate

Monday to Friday, 9:00 a.m. to 12:00 p.m.

Purpose

To help students develop the English-communication skills necessary to succeed in an academic setting.

Approach

Students will be introduced to the topics, grammar points, and vocabulary words featured in the *New Interchange* textbook.

As much as possible, the class will be conversation based. Students are required to participate in pair activities, group discussions, and role plays. Students will also develop their listening, reading, and writing skills. A variety of resources will be used to reinforce what students have learned.

Journals

• 10 minutes per day (submitted on Fridays)

Course work

• Textbook exercises and activities
• Quizzes
• Student-led communication sessions (presentations) on Fridays

Timed writing

• 10- to 15-minute timed writing sessions (Mondays and Wednesdays)
• Group editing

Evaluation

• Term test (fourth Thursday of the term)
• Report card given on final Friday of the term

SAMPLE 26
STUDENT EVALUATION FORM

Student Evaluation Form

Student's name_____ Teacher_____

Term_____ Class_____

Effort and improvement	/20
Speaking (fluency, accuracy, pronunciation)	/20
Listening comprehension	/20
Reading comprehension	/20
Writing (organization, grammar, punctuation)	/20
Overall skills and abilities	Mark /100

Comments:

Teacher's signature_____ Date_____

ENGLISH COMMUNICATION PROGRAM

ABC Institute's English Communication Program

Program Description

ABC Institute's English Communication Program (ECP) is a 12-week program designed to help students increase their speaking speed and accuracy. Three themes are introduced over the course of the program (see below). At the beginning of each four-week term, the teacher and students decide upon a theme that matches the students' needs and interests. Course materials are drawn from a range of sources: textbooks, the Internet, newspapers, books, everyday items, television, videos, songs, brochures, etc.

During Week 1, students focus on **A** (About me)

- Identifying what they already know/believe about the subject
- Vocabulary building
- Related idioms, expressions

During Week 2, students focus on **E** (Experience)

- Expressing their experiences with the subject
- Related grammar
- Pronunciation and linking

During Week 3, students focus on **I** (Information)

- Learning new information about the subject
- Understanding and organizing ideas, and different views on a subject
- Reading and writing

During Week 4, students focus on **O** (Opinion)

- Articulating and expressing opinions about the subject
- Effective communication strategies and techniques
- Presenting, debating, and testing

Term Plan

	Monday	Tuesday	Wednesday	Thursday	Friday
Week 1: **A**	Theme: GTKY*	Vocabulary	Idioms	Expressions	Articulation practice
Week 2: **E**	Discuss experiences	Grammar	Grammar	Linking	Test linking/ grammar
Week 3: **I**	New info (reading)	New info (speaking)	New info (writing)	New info (listening)	New info wrap-up
Week 4: **O**	Articulate opinions	Communication strategies	Debate/ present	Term evaluation	Wrap-up

*GTKY: Getting to Know You exercises/needs assessment

USING ART AS A PROGRAM THEME

Beginner students can do the following:

- Learn about types of art (painting, photography, writing, dance)
- Learn art-related vocabulary (colors, idioms involving colors, adjectives involving the senses)
- Study artists' lives (dates, simple present/past, present continuous)
- Visit a local gallery

Intermediate students can do the following:

- Learn art-related vocabulary and idioms
- Discuss the purpose of art, making cross-cultural comparisons
- Role-play conversations in a theater, art gallery, or bookstore
- Give presentations on art or artists
- Participate in a Q&A session with a local artist

Advanced students can do the following:

- Discuss art history and themes
- Discuss controversies in the art world
- Conduct interviews with local artists
- Attend artists' presentations

Chapter 12

SERVICES

While a school's programs are of primary concern to students, there are other services that play an important role in attracting customers to a particular school. The most important service is arranging accommodation. Less important, but still worth noting, are the extracurricular activities a school offers.

ACCOMMODATION

Student accommodation arrangements are fundamental to a school's success. If students are not comfortable or satisfied with where they are living, they will have difficulty settling into school life. This is especially true for students who are overseas for the first time. Disliking their living situation will exacerbate their homesickness, and they may simply head back home, taking their tuition fees with them.

While it is not always necessary to offer accommodation services, many schools have an in-house department devoted to helping students find a place to live. This is because prospective students often consider programs and accommodation equally when deciding on a school. The more convenient it is to settle into both the school and a suitable living arrangement, the more likely it is that a student will choose that school. Accommodation options are usually homestay or a furnished apartment.

Accommodation services themselves do not generate a great deal of money — typically, a school will simply receive a placement fee in the case of a homestay, and a finder's fee in the case of an apartment. However, simply having in-house accommodation services will help a school attract and retain students.

Some larger cities have separate homestay organizations and apartment-rental companies. In these cities, schools can get away with not having in-house accommodation services. Instead, a school can develop a relationship with a reputable accommodation business and post a link to that business on the school website. In smaller cities or places where accommodation services do not exist, a school must provide accommodation services if it hopes to attract and keep students.

Homestay

Homestay refers to room and board in a family home, with attention and empathy added to the mix. A good homestay family is one that provides the basics — a furnished bedroom and three meals a day — and spends quality time with the student, making him or her feel important and loved, like part of the family.

The typical homestay fee is between US$550 and US$750 per month, depending on the size of the town and the age of the student. Homestay families in larger centers tend to receive more money than their small-town counterparts because of higher living costs. And hosts of school-age children enrolled in the public-school system typically earn more money than those who host adults because of added responsibilities (e.g., ensuring homework is done) and added services (e.g., transportation to and from school or friends' houses).

Students choose homestay for a variety of reasons, including safety, comfort, convenience, and the opportunity to interact with native English speakers. Many parents prefer that their young adult child lives in a controlled, family atmosphere. In many countries, people live with their parents well into adulthood. Unlike many North Americans in their early 20s, international students often want to participate in family activities, and like the idea of bonding with a family.

Matching a student to the right family can be challenging. There are many factors to consider when placing a student, such as food preferences, location in relation to the school, presence of children and pets, shared interests, and the family's availability for social interaction.

Among the most important homestay factors are food, friendliness, and focus on English practice. Students are not always comfortable expressing their true feelings about the type and quantity of food offered. They may feel shy about asking for different items or additional helpings. It is important for homestay hosts to understand that they may have to work to understand their students' likes, dislikes, and cultural differences.

Many students suffer from loneliness and homesickness while overseas. They crave attention, encouragement, and the feeling that they are cared for. Sometimes homestay hosts give their students too much space, mistakenly believing they are similar to North American youth in their desire for independence and freedom. As a result, students sometimes feel ignored and undervalued. Hosts need to know how to gauge their students' needs for both attention and independence.

Students often complain about not having enough opportunities to practice speaking English with their homestay hosts. Sometimes hosts are simply too busy with their work, family concerns, and free-time activities to spend sufficient time with their students. And sometimes the students themselves are painfully shy, making the host feel uncomfortable about engaging in conversation. Hosts need to understand that part of their job is to spend time with their student — even if it is only one hour a day of undivided attention. They also need to know that most international students, however shy, want to be drawn out of their shell. They want to be forced to use their skills, even though they may not seem that keen on conversation.

Because students are paying "rent," they have certain expectations of their homestay hosts. Anything less will make them feel that the family is only interested in the money, rather than the experience of living with a person from another culture. In some cases, this is true — hosts have been known to avoid their homestay duties while happily being paid. The result of this kind of homestay match is usually ugly. The student wants to leave, but will not always express this or even understand exactly why they feel this way. The hosts feel confused, underappreciated, and insulted.

When a student has a problem with a homestay arrangement, it can mean extra work for the school in relocating the student. And there is damage control to be done: students talk openly about negative accommodation experiences. The unfavorable situation of one may cause other students to question their own situations.

Students' problems with accommodation invariably lead to them having problems in school. Students may be depressed or preoccupied, and therefore unable to concentrate in class. They may lean on other students for support, creating a bigger issue that requires intervention by school administrators. In extreme cases, students may want to return to their home countries, and they may demand a refund of their tuition fees.

Because students' level of happiness outside of school affects their mood and behavior when they are at school, it is vital to make good matches of students and homestay families. The role of the school is to secure relationships with homestay families who fully understand and accept their responsibilities as hosts. Doing this requires the school to have clearly defined policies and procedures around becoming and maintaining a designation as a homestay family. Support and encouragement are also necessary for new homestay families who are struggling with cultural differences or have concerns.

The best way to convey your expectations to homestay families is to create a policies and procedures manual. The manual should include the following information:

- Background information
  - About your school: mission statement, programs, services, activities
  - About your students: ages, interests, countries of origin, purpose for studying English
- Homestay information
  - Definition of what hosting a homestay student involves
  - Key roles and responsibilities of hosts
  - Must-haves — private room (including bed, dresser, desk, lamp), three meals a day, located on a bus route (30-minute maximum commute to school)
  - Tentative plan for how the host will spend time and engage in activities with the international student

- Homestay application form for host families
  - Location and contact information
  - Information about family members
  - Reason for wanting to host an international student
  - Details of available room
  - Guest preferences: age, sex, interests
  - House insurance
- Homestay site visit checklist
  - Location — distance from school, bus route
  - Clean and safe
  - Furnished room
  - Host understands roles and responsibilities
- Homestay house rules
  - Time the student is expected to come home at night
  - Shower and bathroom times
  - Telephone use
  - Computer use
  - Visitors and overnight guests
  - Rules regarding keys and locking doors and windows
- Homestay contract (signed by homestay host and student)
  - Outlines roles and responsibilities
  - Specifies payment details
  - Lays out house rules
  - Identifies procedures in the event of problems or breaking the contract
- Homestay-payment fee schedule
  - Monthly fee
  - Payment dates, times, and places
- Support-network sheet
  - Contact information in the event of problems
  - How to interpret and/or deal with cross-cultural differences

You can develop your own homestay application form and policies or use the ones provided in Samples 29, 30, and 31.

Apartment rentals

For students who wish to live independently, you may want to offer help finding a suitable furnished apartment or basement suite. In some cases this may be difficult, given that students tend to stay for short periods of time — typically three to six months. Still, developing relationships with apartment rental companies will at least provide you with options for your students.

Some schools discourage students from living in apartments with other students, particularly those who come from the same country or speak the same language. Students who speak their native language outside school have more difficulty developing their English skills and may become depressed. Some even blame the school's programs or teachers for their lack of success at learning English.

A better option is to match students with people from other countries. Better yet, match them with North Americans needing a roommate.

HOMESTAY APPLICATION FORM (for students)

ABC Institute Homestay Student Application Form

Date of Application_____

Personal Information

Surname (Family Name)	Given Names	English Name
Sex [ ] Male [ ] Female	Date of Birth (month/day/year)	Age
First Language		Other Languages Spoken

Home Address

Street Address			
City	State/Province	Country	Postal Code
Telephone (home and cell)	Fax		E-mail

Parents' Information

Father's Surname	First Name	Occupation
Mother's Surname	First Name	Occupation

Other Family Members

Name	Male/Female	Relationship	Age

General Information

1. Do you want to live with a family that has pets?   [   ] Yes   [   ] No   [   ] No preference

2. Do you prefer a home that is: [   ] Nonsmoking   [   ] Smoking   [   ] No preference

3. Do you have any special dietary requirements (e.g., Are you a vegetarian)?   [   ] Yes   [   ] No
    If yes, please list preferred sources of protein: _____

4. What foods do you like to eat?

   What foods do you dislike?

5. How would you feel about being placed in a home with children who are older or younger than you, or a home that has no children?

6. What are your activities/hobbies? (please check all that apply)

   [   ] Sports   [   ] Theater

   [   ] Music   [   ] Dance

   [   ] Art   [   ] Computer/Internet

   [   ] Cooking   [   ] Exercise/fitness

7. What is your religion? (optional)_____

8. How often do you attend religious services? (optional)_____

9. Please describe any part-time jobs or work experience you have had.

10. Do you usually help with household chores?   [   ] Yes   [   ] No

    If yes, please describe which ones:

11. Have you ever been away from your family for a long period of time?

    [   ] Yes   [   ] No   If yes, for how long?_____

12. Describe any concerns you have about living in North America:

13. How can we help you adjust to your new home?

14. Describe any medical conditions your homestay family should be aware of:

15. Do you have any serious or life-threatening medical conditions that may require immediate medical attention?

[   ] Yes   [   ] No   [   ] If yes, please describe:

16. Please provide any further information you feel would be useful in helping us to place you in the best possible homestay setting.

HOMESTAY APPLICATION FORM (for host families)

ABC Institute Homestay Host Family Application Form

Date_____

Contact information

Applicant's Name_____

Address_____

City_____ Zip Code/Postal Code_____

Home phone_____ Work phone_____

Cell phone_____ E-mail_____

People who live in your home

Name	School/Occupation	Date of Birth	Relationship to you

1. (Applicant)_____

2._____

3._____

4._____

5._____

Have you ever hosted an international student in your home?   [   ] Yes   [   ] No

If yes, please provide details:

Nationality	Sex/Age	School/Agency	When	Length of Stay

_____

_____

_____

_____

_____

Do you prefer a student who is: [   ] Female   [   ] Male   [   ] No preference

About your home

Style of home: [   ] House   [   ] Townhouse   [   ] Apartment

Number of Bedrooms_____   Number of Bathrooms_____

Pets_____

Special foods or diets_____

House rules_____

Family's interests and hobbies_____

Transportation

Name and number of nearest bus_____

Travel time to ESL school_____

I have attached:

[   ] Two reference letters

[   ] A criminal record check for all adults (necessary for hosting students younger than 19 years old)

[   ] A copy of my house insurance with $1 million in liability coverage.

I have read and understood the criteria set out in *Homestay Family Policies and Guidelines*. I accept its terms and conditions.

_____   _____
Signature of Applicant   Date

_____
Print name of Applicant

_____   _____
Signature of Applicant   Date

_____
Print name of Applicant

SAMPLE 31
HOMESTAY POLICIES

ABC Institute Homestay Policies

Accommodation

Room: Private room with window, closet, and smoke detector

Furniture: Bed and bedding, dresser, mirror, desk, chair, lamp

Bathroom: Easy to access, with a locking door

Laundry: Facilities accessible to student

Meals: All food is provided by host family. Student is responsible for preparing his or her own breakfast and lunch. Dinner should be a hot meal prepared by the host family. Dinnertime should be a time when family members and student spend time together. In the case of the host family's absence during dinner time, student must be informed in advance. Arrangements must be made to ensure student is properly fed.

Activities: Host family and student should spend some free time together. Activity expenses should be paid for by host family.

Fees

Host family will receive a cheque for $750 ($25 per day) on the first day of each month from ABC Institute.

Expectations of Host Parents

Orientation: Help student unpack and get settled. Show student around the home and orient student to home equipment.

Emergencies: Give student your daytime contact information. Ask student to carry this information at all times. Explain to student how to remain safe and what to do in an emergency situation such as a fire.

Communication: Speak English at all times in the home. As often as possible, spend time talking with the student. If communication difficulties arise, contact ABC Institute's homestay-program coordinator.

Chores/Duties: Create a list of house responsibilities and discuss them with the student.

House Rules: Create a list of house rules to ensure mutual understanding of mealtimes, bedtimes, laundry schedule, times for incoming phone calls in the evening, time limits for bathroom use, etc.

Insurance: Homeowners must have a minimum of $1 million liability coverage.

Moving and Cancellations

Students must give one month's notice in writing before moving out. If a student moves out sooner, the host family will still be paid the full month's fee. If a family fails to meet homestay requirements, ABC Institute reserves the right to terminate the homestay arrangement. If cancellation occurs before the end of the month, the homestay family must pay back the remainder of the month's fees.

EXTRACURRICULAR ACTIVITIES

After-school activities are important for helping students in your school bond. Through activities, students get a chance to interact with one another in a more relaxed, social setting. And when they are not divided into academic levels, they have a chance to meet students from different classes.

Students usually enjoy having teachers and school staff participate in after-school activities. With native English speakers present, students are less likely to fall back into the habit of using their own languages. As well, students and staff get the chance to be on a more equal footing. They can get to know each other as people, rather than as the roles they play within the school environment.

While not as important as programs or homestay in a student's decision to attend a particular school, activities play a part in a student's perception of the overall experience they have while overseas. Schools that appear to be fun and active, besides offering high-quality academic classes, are more attractive than schools that do not offer social opportunities. This is especially true for shy students who want and need to be encouraged to interact with others.

Many schools offer activities on Friday afternoon (classes often end for the week at noon on Friday). Some schools offer additional activities during the week or even on weekends. A typical activity lasts two to four hours. However, some last all day or, in the case of camping, overnight.

The activities offered depend on the city, season, and even the weather.

On-site indoor activities could include —

- watching a movie,
- playing board games,
- learning how to cook a special dish,
- participating in a dance or martial arts class,
- holding a music jam session, and
- doing arts and crafts.

Off-site indoor activities could include —

- visiting a museum or art gallery;
- participating in an art or music workshop;
- doing volunteer work at a local organization;
- taking a tour of an unusual place, such as a TV station or brewery;
- going swimming or skating at a recreation center;
- going bowling; and
- holding a billiards tournament.

Outdoor activities might include —

- playing an organized sport — golf, soccer, tennis, baseball, etc.;
- going swimming or cycling;
- going hiking or rock climbing;
- taking scuba diving lessons;
- going jet skiing or tubing;
- attending an outdoor sporting event — baseball game, football game, etc.;
- participating in a treasure hunt or fact-finding mission; and

- visiting an outdoor market.

Weekend trips and excursions might include —

- camping,
- sightseeing in a neighboring city,
- going on a nature tour,
- going on a special shopping trip to a famously fashionable place, and
- attending a concert or event in another city.

In order for an activity to be successful, it has to be well organized. Nothing is worse for school morale than a much-anticipated activity failing to get off the ground because of poor organization, miscommunication between staff members, or a lack of attention to details.

Students need to know well in advance what the activity is, and when and where it will be held. They also need to be clearly informed of the cost (if any), as well as when to pay and the preferred method of payment. One way to do this is to post fliers and sign-up sheets at the school, advertising the proposed event.

To ensure that students participate in activities, it is a good idea to request suggestions for activities from the students themselves. Even taking an informal poll during class can help staff choose wisely.

Not all students have a lot of spending money, which means some students may not be able to participate in expensive activities and excursions. For this reason, it is wise to choose less expensive (or even free) activities as the mainstays of your activities program.

Generally speaking, students don't like the idea of spending additional money in order to be part of the group. More expensive trips should be offered only once every one or two months. Students should be given ample notice so that they can find a way to get extra money if they want to participate.

Chapter  13

KEY PEOPLE AND THEIR ROLES

Having a solid team in place before you open your school will help you get through the initial "growing pains" period of your business. You need to have the right people on board to both launch your school and help you achieve early success. But who are the right people? And what roles will they play?

Because the ESL industry is dynamic and somewhat unpredictable, on your team you need to have high-energy people who are comfortable with change. Almost every role in an ESL business requires strong organizational skills and adaptability. For example, as a teacher you may have four students in your class one day and seven the next. As a home-stay coordinator, one day all of your students may be placed in good homes, and the next day you may receive three requests for relocation. As a program coordinator, you may be

faced with a group of students requesting programs not currently offered by your school. High-energy people who easily adapt to change can handle such situations without batting an eye.

You also need people who understand that your school is a business, and that your students are, in essence, customers. If some members of your team think otherwise, you could have problems moving forward. For example, teachers who are accustomed to the public school system may not be used to students playing a role in deciding what is taught or how something is taught. They may be uncomfortable with the idea that their role is not to "educate" their students, but to "serve" them and teach them what they agreed to pay for, which most often amounts to the opportunity to practice speaking English.

98

To avoid battles over what ESL education means, you are best off choosing team members who readily understand and accept the "students as customers" model. You will also want to clarify each team member's key roles and responsibilities.

In large schools, each staff member plays one key role: the director directs business matters, teachers teach, the marketer sells the school's programs to overseas agents and students. But in smaller operations, especially in the case of start-up schools, staff members often have multiple roles.

Regardless of the size and scope of your school, you need clearly defined job descriptions for each member of your team. As your business changes and develops, the roles and responsibilities may change. Still, conveying what is expected of your team before you open your doors will go a long way to avoid unnecessary headaches and confusion over who is responsible for particular tasks.

This chapter describes seven of the key roles in an ESL business.

DIRECTOR

Your director is effectively the official face of your school, the person responsible for handling all public relations and legal matters. The director also oversees the daily operations of the business. He or she is the person with the final word on human resources, program planning and development, policy making and enforcement, and financial matters.

A good director demonstrates strong organizational, management, and social skills. Ideally, your director would hold a postgraduate degree in a business-related field and have a thorough understanding of the ESL

industry. Teaching experience in the ESL industry would be also an asset.

PROGRAM COORDINATOR

Your program coordinator is responsible for the smooth operation of classes. This means determining which programs to run each term, deciding who should teach individual courses, and choosing which students to put in a particular class.

Another part of the program coordinator's role concerns teacher management. They are responsible for ensuring that teachers are clear about their roles and comfortable with the classes they are teaching. Teachers also need to understand what to do and where to seek help if problems arise in the classroom.

A good program coordinator has strong organizational, analytical, and problem-solving skills. Your ideal program coordinator would have a degree and several years of teaching experience in the private ESL-school system.

TEACHERS

Your teachers can make or break your school, so having likable, effective teachers on staff is vital. Besides providing English language instruction, your teachers are responsible for ensuring that students want to stay at your school for the length of time they have registered for (as opposed to moving to another school). When students extend their stay at your school, you can be confident that your teachers (and homestay families) are doing a good job.

To keep students interested in their classes, teachers must be lively, energetic, and skilled at explaining grammar points and definitions of terms clearly and precisely. Teachers must also be able to easily monitor their classes for warning signs — the pace is too fast or too slow, problems are developing between students, the content is not appropriate for the group's long-term goals — and solve problems swiftly.

Ideally, all teachers would have overseas teaching experience. Knowing what it feels like to live and work in another country goes a long way toward understanding students' experiences studying overseas. Additionally, knowing how and what students are required to study in their home countries helps a teacher better understand student expectations and perceptions.

Looking back, it was my overseas experience that taught me how to be most effective in the classroom. My teaching job in South Korea was very chaotic — I worked early mornings and late nights, and I had screeching five-year-olds in one class and serious businesspeople in the next class ten minutes later. Sometimes my boss would give me two days' notice before I had to teach a special short-term program that I would be required to plan, develop, and implement. While it was stressful at the time, my overseas experience taught me how to be quick on my feet and forced me to create a "bag of tricks" that I could use in situations where I had few teaching resources available, or had miscalculated the timing and was finished my lesson 20 minutes before the class was scheduled to end. Being able to handle chaos and last-minute changes or developments is a skill that makes teaching ESL both bearable and enjoyable.

Regarding formal qualifications, there is some flexibility in the industry. In California, for example, teachers who want to teach a credit program at a community college must have a minimum of a bachelor's degree in TESL or TESOL, or English with a TESL certificate. When it comes to Intensive English Programs, requirements vary by institution, as there are no national qualifications in the US or Canada. The general rule is that teachers must have a master's degree in TESOL or Applied Linguistics, plus overseas experience. However, there is often room for "equivalents," meaning some teachers can get by with a combination of education and experience.

In the United States and Canada, steps have been taken to standardize credentials. In practical terms, this usually means a school cannot join an industry association unless its teachers have a certain level of education and experience. Not being part of an association means losing out on key marketing opportunities and industry events. However, the reality is that formal credentials do not make a good teacher. (In my experience, the teachers with the most education are the least effective teachers.) And when your school is small, everything depends on your students' classroom experience. You need the right teachers for your business, and this often has nothing to do with education.

Some schools request that prospective employees teach mock classes as part of the interview process. You and your team can be the "students" if you do not have students on hand to participate in a practice class.

MARKETER

Your marketer is the person who ensures that there is a continuous flow of students entering your school. The marketer does this by making connections with local and overseas agents, attending education fairs, networking with other schools, and even drawing upon useful personal contacts.

Because a large part of marketing is word-of-mouth advertising, the marketer may also be responsible for staying aware of the concerns of current students. Knowing which aspects of the school are satisfying to students — good teachers, useful courses, interesting extracurricular activities — provides the marketer with the first-hand knowledge and testimonials needed to interest new students and agents.

Being in a position to interact openly with students, the marketer also has a chance to find out what aspects of the school experience are less than satisfying to students. This information can be passed on to the administration and teachers, giving the team an opportunity to solve problems. When students are happy (and know that their concerns are both acknowledged and addressed in a timely fashion), they are sure to pass on a good word about the school, thus lightening the marketing load and greatly reducing expenses.

To do an effective job of marketing, the marketer needs to have the information and material expected of a reputable institution. That is, the marketer needs a marketing package containing program and schedule information, background blurbs on the teachers and staff, homestay and activities information, write-ups about the location and nearby attractions, and contact information, preferably in the form of a business card that includes the website and e-mail addresses. Your marketing material and website must be in place and professional-looking before you can expect agents or education-fair representatives to take your school seriously.

School owners who are reluctant to spend money on marketing invariably lose out on opportunities to attract students. It is inadvisable to create brochures, rack cards, or business cards on your home computer. It is better to spend your time gathering and organizing the information that needs to be included in the marketing materials and handing the job over to someone who specializes in design and printing services.

A good marketer is persuasive. But more importantly, a marketer should be a person whom people find trustworthy. An ESL-school marketer bears a great deal of pressure since students call the marketer on things that are amiss at the school. For example, if the programs advertised are not the same as those offered by the school, the marketer may be the person who is blamed for the misinformation.

Ideally, your marketer speaks multiple languages — English and one or more of the languages spoken by your core group of students — and has a number of key education-related contacts in place. Please see Chapter 15 for more information on marketing.

ACCOMMODATION COORDINATOR

The role of an accommodation coordinator is to match students with a suitable living arrangement during their overseas stay. Doing this job well means getting to know the needs, desires, and budgets of individual students.

For students wanting to live independently, the accommodation coordinator needs to have an up-to-date list of available apartments and furnished suites, as well as a solid relationship with landlords.

An accommodation coordinator also matches international students with suitable homestay families. To find the right fit, the coordinator must be able to understand the needs and desires of individual students, as well as convey the value to local homeowners of sharing their space and family time with a stranger from another country and culture.

Being an accommodation coordinator requires strong organizational and interpersonal skills. Patience and understanding are also needed at times, since students often request moves to alternative homestays for reasons that are not always clear or easily understood by staff.

Homestay is such an important part of the overall ESL experience that selecting the best accommodation coordinator is crucial. The person needs to be tough enough to deal with the occasional bruised ego or particularly picky student, as well as sensitive and persuasive enough to reassure all parties that their concerns will be both heard and addressed. For more information on accommodation services, see Chapter 12.

OFFICE STAFF

Depending on the size of your business, your office staff may include a receptionist or secretary. As the frontline person, your receptionist or secretary should be friendly, courteous, well organized, and experienced at communicating with people from other countries. It can be difficult to understand students and overseas representatives with heavy accents and minimal English skills, so patience and a sense of humor are necessary.

Your office staff may also include a bookkeeper, preferably one with some knowledge of the ESL industry. Larger, more complicated businesses may decide to hire an accountant (see Chapter 19).

ACTIVITIES STAFF

The people who run your activities need to be well organized and able to coordinate schedules and motivate students. It can be difficult to encourage participation among students who are not accustomed to taking time away from their busy schedules to engage in fun. For this reason, your activities staff should be lively and outgoing, spreading excitement and interest in the scheduled activity. Another necessary trait in activities staff is compassion for students who dislike or fear strenuous or challenging outdoor activities.

Chapter 14

LOCATION AND FACILITIES

Some school owners find the perfect location for their school and then create programs that suit the locale. Others determine the type of school they want to operate and search for the right location. Still others keep a close eye on industry trends and choose a place and programs accordingly.

Whichever method you use when selecting a location, be sure you are clear about your target market. What kinds of students will your location attract? How many other schools in the area are competing for those same students? If you are opening your school in a smaller community, how far is your town from a major center? How far away is the closest international airport?

URBAN VERSUS RURAL

By and large, students who study overseas are city dwellers used to the clamor of buses and trains, honking horns, and traffic jams. They are often more comfortable in large urban areas because they are used to the bustle and nightlife. However, many students are aware that large cities are expensive places to study, not to mention full of people who speak the students' native languages. The trend toward smaller, safer, English-speaking towns is growing. More and more students are choosing to study in places where they are forced to speak English for the simple reason that few other languages are used in the area.

But it is not always easy to market a small town to students, and building a reputation as a valuable business, equal or greater to schools found in cities, takes time, patience, and hard work. It also takes a marketing angle. Why should international students leave the "comfort and convenience" of the city for your small-town school? Is there something special about your school, programs, or location?

Going the small-town route may indeed be worth the effort, especially if you are one of those city-weary entrepreneurs who prefers the quality of life in smaller centers. But be warned: Just because *you* like the slower pace and the great outdoors does not mean your potential students do too. More than one ESL operation has been ruined because the owner assumed that everyone wants a relaxing atmosphere in which to study, and a location that offers great hiking, rock climbing, and scuba diving. Indeed, some students dislike physical activity of any kind. Most students who come to North America want to exercise their minds and their mouths, by speaking English with native English speakers. You are better off finding a location that will guarantee your students get to meet and socialize with English speakers of the same age.

LOCATION GUIDELINES

Whether you are planning to open a city-based school or one in a small town, consider the needs, wants, and perceptions of your target market. Also keep in mind the following location guidelines.

If you are opening your school in a city, you should choose the following:

- A location that has English-speaking homestay hosts in the neighborhood (30 minutes away or less by bus or subway) and available apartments close by.
- A building in a safe, aesthetically pleasing part of town, where public transportation is readily available.

If you are opening your school in a smaller center, you should choose the following:

- A town that is less than a two-hour drive from a major airport.
- A town that has shopping centers and other city-like attractions less than an hour's drive away.
- A town where people are not xenophobic (fearful of foreigners).
- A building that is located in the center of town or on major bus routes (which should link the school to homestay homes).

Your facilities must include the following:

- An office and office equipment
- Classrooms
- A computer room
- A lounge or eating area
- Restrooms (enough to accommodate your students and staff)

You might also consider having a staff room, meeting room, or counseling room.

Chapter **15**

MARKETING

Effective marketing is the only way to keep your school thriving. Besides having the right person in charge of "selling" your school (see Chapter 13), you need the right marketing tools and the right connections. Once your school is off the ground, you need "happy customers" who will post on the Internet about how wonderful your institution is.

PROMOTIONAL MATERIAL

In order to "win" students through an agent or at an education fair, your marketer will need evidence that your school is a quality institution worth attending. For this reason, your promotional materials should, at the very least, consist of a high-end website and professionally made brochures. Good-quality business cards are also a must.

Your promotional packages should contain some of the following items:

- Brochures

- Business cards

- Detailed program information

- A list of costs

- Homestay information

- Description of the town or city and what it has to offer in terms of entertainment, activities, and unique features

- Testimonials from students, as evidence of a positive experience

Because students have many schools to choose from, your marketing materials need to stand out. They should also match the perceptions of your market. Students cannot be expected to feel confident about a school that tries to save money on marketing materials by cobbling together its own website, brochures, and business cards. What's more, your marketer will have a difficult time convincing agents and trade show visitors that your school is a serious business.

Photos are an effective way to convey what your school is like. Use photos to show the type of school you are running. Try to include "action" shots — students participating in a fun classroom activity, teachers engaged in an emphatic explanation of a key grammar point, staff and students enjoying a picnic on the beach or an interesting excursion. Avoid using shots of scenery that don't include people. And be sure to include photos showing students of different nationalities mixing and communicating with one another.

A key point about language: your marketing materials must be written in easy-to-understand English. Ideally, you would also offer versions in other languages to ensure that students at the beginner level understand what your school offers and why they should choose your programs and services.

AGENTS

Agents are people who have key connections to overseas institutions and student groups. Agents act as networkers — students seek advice from them about where to travel and which school to attend, while schools strive to get on their list of places to study.

Most students prefer to use agents rather than take the risk of applying directly to an ESL school. This is because students like the idea of someone being accountable for their travel and study concerns. They also like the

idea of having one person in charge of handling their fees, both school and homestay related.

Agents receive a commission from every student they place at a school. While some agents charge as much as 50 percent of a student's tuition, most agents are more reasonable. The average commission is 20 percent to 30 percent.

Working with agents can be costly, but it is often necessary when you are first starting out. The first order of business for any new school is getting students through the doors and into the classroom, if for no other reason than to legitimize its existence. (Students feel uncomfortable being in a school that has too few students.)

WORD-OF-MOUTH ADVERTISING

Letting your students sell your school for you is the easiest and cheapest form of marketing. It is also the best way to guarantee your school will stay profitable for years to come. Once students start saying positive things to their friends, parents, and agents about your programs and teachers, your business will quickly develop a reputation that draws in more students.

Thanks to the Internet, students around the world are connected to one another. And they do talk, sharing both the good and bad of their overseas experiences. For this reason, it is vital that you understand, respect, and value your students as customers. If they like you, your team, and what you are offering in terms of programs and services, you will need to spend less on advertising than you think.

But how can you rely on word-of-mouth advertising when there are no "mouths" in your classrooms yet? That is, how do you get students into your school to begin with? In an ideal world, you and each member of your team would bring to the table connections with former students and other people in the ESL industry. Letting everyone you know, or have known and can get in touch with, about your new business can help you get the ball rolling. These people can help you by talking to students they know about you, your team, and your school's programs. It is easy for them to spread the word through e-mail and student-oriented chat rooms. Having people who like you and believe in your future will help you sell your school idea in an effective and inexpensive way during the early days of your business.

PROMOTIONS

Promotions, or "deals," can help pull in your first batch of students, or kick off a slow start to a usually busy or especially competitive season. Some schools offer discounts, such as "Fifty percent off the registration fee if you sign up for three months of classes" or "Pay for two months and get the third month for half price." Others offer special deals for referring other students. For example, "One week of free classes for every student referral who registers."

While most people like the idea of saving money, there is a danger to offering promotions, particularly grandiose promotions that promise too much or seem too good to be true. They can be perceived by students and agents as "begging." After all, confident businesses rarely have promotions, presumably because they do not need help in attracting business. If you do choose to go the promotions route, exercise restraint. Choose the timing wisely, and make sure your customers understand the purpose. Keep in mind that in the long run, it is better for your business to be perceived as exclusive, or busy enough to have a waiting list, than so in need of students that you are willing to give your services away for free.

For more information on marketing your ESL school, see *Marketing Your Service*, another title published by Self-Counsel Press.

Chapter 16

POLICIES AND PROCEDURES

To ensure the smooth operation of your school, you need to decide on the "school rules" before you open your doors. That is, you need to have policies and procedures in place so that problems are dealt with swiftly and effectively. Smaller schools in particular have to make a conscious effort to deal with problems in a quick, efficient manner. Discontent and rumors can spread through a school with alarming speed. The longer a problem is allowed to fester, the more damage it can do to the harmony of the school.

What kinds of problems should you be prepared for? Problems vary, and some are harder to solve than others. For example, a student might complain that he or she feels isolated or disliked by classmates. Of course, there is no magic formula that makes one student like another student. However, once

administrators and teachers are aware of the situation, steps can be taken to promote camaraderie between classmates, or at the very least encourage participation in extracurricular activities with host families and other native English speakers.

Problems can arise involving fees and refunds, program and class schedules, or teachers. Ideally, policies should already be in place to resolve any issues that may arise.

Instead of lecturing students about paying their fees on time, or interrogating them about their feelings toward a particular teacher or class, school administrators should direct students to the school's policy book. In an ideal world, students would understand in advance the consequences of not paying fees on time, and students with complaints would know they had the right to voice their concerns, and would be familiar with the school's procedures in dealing with such problems.

COMMON ISSUES WARRANTING A FORMAL POLICY OR PROCEDURE

While some issues in the ESL industry may warrant flexibility, most are predictable. Below is a list of some of the most common problems that arise in ESL schools:

- *Level changes*. Some students are uncomfortable when they feel they are at a higher (or lower) level than the other students in their class. Do you appease the student by moving him or her, or administer a level test to make him or her earn the move?

- *Program changes*. Some students decide mid-program that they want to be in a different program. Do you make them wait until the end of the program, or do you let them transfer right away?

- *Class changes*. Sometimes students have difficulties with classmates or their teacher, preventing them from being able to concentrate in class. Should they be allowed to move, or do you first raise the problem with the students and/or the teacher?

- *Homestay changes*. Sometimes students have problems with their homestay house (too far from the school, not clean enough, insufficient or unsatisfactory food) or their homestay hosts (too quiet, too loud, too many children, too many pets). Should they be permitted to move? If so, is there an extra fee involved?

- *Program cancellation and refunds*. Sometimes students have emergencies, or simply want to go to another school, and wish to have returned the fees they paid in advance. Do you deny the request, pay the student in full, or put in place a graduated policy whereby students receive a full refund in the case of an emergency at home (e.g., a death in the family), 90 percent if cancellation occurs in the first week of classes, and 65 percent in the second week?

- *Continuous intake*. Many schools, smaller ones in particular, allow new students to start classes on any day of the week, at any point during a program. Ushering in a new student during the third week of a four-week class can be disruptive enough to change the environment of the classroom. Do you take the disruptions in stride, or do you make one day a week "intake day"?

- *Fee discrepancies*. Sometimes students discover large discrepancies in the tuition fees they pay, due to promotions and deals offered by different agents. Do you take steps to appease students who find out they are paying more?

- *Students speaking their native language in class or in the school*. Many students find it difficult to speak only English throughout the entire day. Sometimes they spend their free time chatting in their own language, much to the chagrin of students who are spending money to fully immerse themselves in English. You need to decide where and when, if at all, students are permitted to speak their own language. Can they speak their native tongue outside during breaks? What about in the case of an emergency? And what happens if a student is caught speaking his or her own language in the English-only zone? Will they be denied computer privileges or required to do cleanup duties? What if it happens more than once? Should you suspend a student for breaking the rules repeatedly? If so, for how long?

- *A group of students dominating the computer lab or students skipping classes to use the computer.* Some students cannot seem to unglue themselves from the computer. Shy students sometimes cling to the computer to avoid having to communicate with real people, while others simply enjoy sending e-mail and surfing the Net. What happens if the same group of students is always on the computers, while others have to wait their turn? Do you have a time limit for computer use? If so, how is it monitored? And what do you do about students who choose the computer room over the classroom? On a similar note, is there a rule regarding students scanning disks for viruses, or downloading material, or printing off documents on the school's printer?

Your policies and procedures should be written in easy-to-understand English. Use simple vocabulary and short sentences where possible.

Take a look at the policies and procedures related to program and classroom changes in Sample 32.

PREPARING FOR FUTURE POLICY AND PROCEDURE ISSUES

As your school gets off the ground, issues are likely to arise that you could not have foreseen. The trick is to make sure that problems that come your way are noticed and dealt with coolly, rather than emotionally.

Here are two issues that have taken school owners by surprise:

- Theft of electronic dictionaries, MP3 players, and other items belonging to students

- Overflowing toilets as a result of female students attempting to flush away sanitary napkins

Think of the best way to prevent the problems from happening again, convey to students the new policy and procedure, and move on.

PROGRAM AND CLASSROOM POLICIES

ABC Institute Program and Classroom Policies

ABC Institute wants every student to enjoy his or her overseas study experience. To make sure all students enjoy their classes and activities, we have made a list of program and classroom policies.

New students

New students are welcome *on the first day of a new term* (each term is four weeks long). New students take a speaking and writing test to determine their language level. They also talk to the program coordinator about the program they want to take. New students start classes the following day. When they arrive, they are given a class schedule.

Program changes

Students can change programs *when a new term begins*. Students must talk to the program coordinator about the change at least one week before the new term starts.

Class changes

Students can change classes *during the first week of a new term*. Students should first talk to the teacher to see if the problem can be resolved. Students who still want to move must ask the teacher for a class change form, which is filled out and given to the program director. The following day, the student will be given a new schedule.

Level changes

Students move up a level when their teacher feels they are ready. Students can challenge a teacher's decision by taking a level test and scoring 80 percent or higher. Students wanting to schedule a level test should talk to the program coordinator.

Chapter 17

MAINTAINING AND BUILDING YOUR CUSTOMER BASE

Imagine you are up and running, with a big-picture plan and a curriculum in place, and a core group of students in classes taught by high-quality instructors. What comes next? How do you keep your students happy and fulfilled? How do you get them to tell their friends about what you and your team have to offer?

Besides obvious practices related to treating students as customers — for example, being aware of your students' needs, desires, and perceptions, and making sure your programs fit your market — there are several small things you can do to keep your student base strong and ever-expanding.

In the ESL world, little things can mean a lot. While a small problem can escalate into a big problem if it is not handled properly, small gestures can go a long way toward creating a school atmosphere that is envied by students in other institutions.

LITTLE PROBLEMS THAT CAN TURN INTO BIG PROBLEMS

Little problems are things about your school or staff that your students might find odd, uncomfortable, or unjust. Students usually accept small inconveniences or things they do not really like when overall they are satisfied with the school. That is, they will not complain about small problems if they like their instructors and feel that what they are learning in class is valuable.

Some school owners fail to recognize or acknowledge that certain characteristics of their school may work against their success. The location may be somewhat inconvenient for students to access, for example. Some school owners do not understand enough about their market to anticipate potential problems with the school. But wise owners know they must continually strive to understand how their facilities, decisions, and actions are perceived by their market. They also know that students will only put up with a certain number of little problems before losing faith in or patience with a school.

Below are some of the things school owners need to keep under control if they want to keep small problems small.

Cutting corners

All business owners want to keep their expenses down. After all, what is the use of buying expensive classroom furniture or office supplies if they are not necessary? Why pay a teacher $30 per hour if you can get away with paying $20?

Cutting corners is fine if the end result is truly the same as it would be with the more expensive furniture or the more highly paid teacher. The problem is that more often than not, cheap furniture does not look very good, nor does it last long. The same goes for supplies. Buying wipe board markers from the dollar store may seem like a good idea, but are you really saving money if they only last a few days?

Cutting corners with staff is even more risky. Some schools with small budgets luck out and find good teachers who will work for less than they deserve. But they usually do not stick around for very long. Having ineffective teachers on staff will ultimately sink your business. So the question is, Is saving money on the wages of key staff worth it when you consider the high cost of human resources management and the risk involved with hiring inexperienced or incompetent instructors? If you are really serious about your school and want good teachers to help you grow and develop your business, pick professionals and offer them appropriate salaries.

Awkward coffee breaks and lunch breaks

While it may seem trivial, coffee matters. There is nothing quite so annoying and distracting as a school that cannot get its coffee act together. Keeping the coffee flowing is a courtesy and goes a long way toward making a school seem professional.

If a school says it provides students with coffee, there should always be enough supplies on hand, including machines big enough to make a sufficient amount of coffee for the students and staff. Ideally, one person is in charge of maintaining supplies and making coffee before school begins, and before breaks and lunchtime.

Coffee cleanup is often an issue in ESL businesses. Whose job is it to clean up at the end of the day? And what about collecting dirty cups from window sills or wiping up coffee rings left on tables? Some schools try to make students responsible for cleaning up, but the system invariably fails because there are always some people who cooperate and some who do not. While your school should have a cleanup policy in place, it needs to be gently enforced in a way that does not irritate students.

You are better off hiring someone to take care of cleaning up than constantly scolding students for being irresponsible — especially since some will have been following the rules and will therefore be offended.

Nagging

As a school owner, you will regularly be faced with annoyances and issues that need to be dealt with. A common gripe among owners is the mess left by students at breaks and lunchtime. How can you get students to clean up after themselves? Another common problem, especially in larger schools, is the matter of maintaining an English-only policy. How can you ensure that a handful of less serious students do not ruin the English-only experience for the others?

The short answer is that whatever you do, do not nag. Nagging your students — in the form of meetings or notices — will ultimately create disharmony in your school. There will be frustration among the students who are working hard to follow school rules, and for others the information will go in one ear and out the other.

The best way to deal with these small annoyances — which can quickly become big issues — is to find a swift, effective solution. If you cannot get full cooperation from students about cleaning up, spend some money on a janitor or hire a student-run cleanup crew. Or simply do the cleaning up yourself; the money or time you spend solving the problem quickly will save you money and time in the long run. Students pay a great deal of money to study overseas. The last thing they want is to be scolded about non-English matters.

The same principle applies to finding ways of maintaining an English-only facility. In addition to hanging "English-only" signs around the building, some schools "ticket" students for not following the rules — one ticket is a warning, two tickets means missing a day of classes, and three tickets results in expulsion.

While reminding students about the value of using English at all times is almost expected of owners and teachers, lectures on the subject are not necessary. Instead, have a clearly laid out English policy in place and stick to it without making it a huge issue. Students who are expelled for disregarding the policy will pass the word around that your school is serious about its policy.

Too many holidays

Although most adult students expect to attend classes throughout the year, they understand that North American schools close for public holidays. However, few students like it when a school closes "unnecessarily" for an extended period of time, including around Christmas. Many students do not celebrate Christmas, and most have such limited time overseas that they want to make the most of their time there. Additionally, many students — especially new students living and studying in small towns — have little to do when their school is closed. For a student, there is nothing worse than moving to a new country, meeting new people, starting classes, and then having a weeklong break right away. Since students arrive at different times during the course of a term, their schedules should be taken into consideration, or they should be informed about school breaks before they arrive.

If you need to take a break or a holiday, plan far in advance and get trustworthy people to cover for you. Avoid closing the school except on statutory holidays. Even though your students may take breaks during their study period, your school should not appear to need one; some students interpret breaks and holidays as laziness. Being open for business year-round will help your school develop a more serious, hardworking reputation.

Lack of take-home materials

As every school owner knows, textbooks — and the workbooks, tapes, and CDs that accompany them — are expensive. Some owners give out textbooks and workbooks as part of their program, including the costs in the tuition fees. Other schools have class sets, so that the books are used in the classroom and not taken home. In such cases, teachers normally provide students with photocopies of the key material. (If you are providing students with photocopies of materials, make sure you are complying with your country's copyright requirements.) Some schools "rent out" textbooks, making students pay a deposit which is given back when students return their books before heading back to their home country. Other schools develop their own in-house textbooks. This takes a great deal of time — and therefore money — to get off the ground, but in the long run it could save you money, and even lead to the creation of other lucrative materials.

Students expect to take home evidence that they have learned something. This means your school needs to provide them with something, whether it is a textbook they can write in or photocopies of learning materials. Trying to save money by using class sets (and few photocopied materials) may keep your costs down, but it is unwise from a marketing perspective.

Your best bet is to provide students with at least one core textbook, and incorporate the costs into their fees.

LITTLE NICETIES THAT SPREAD GOOD VIBES

In the ideal school, students mill around in the mornings, chatting with one another as they drink their coffee and prepare for class. The atmosphere is calm but cheery. At break time and during lunchtime, students and staff get to know each other, asking questions and sharing experiences. During school, students are satisfied with their programs and teachers, and know that any issues that arise — with their studies, classmates, or homestays — will be dealt with swiftly and efficiently. After school, students make plans to get together to study, socialize, go to a movie, or get some exercise.

In the less-than-ideal school, there is tension between students, as well as between students and staff. Students appear uncomfortable and spend their break times whispering about what is wrong with their classes and homestays. The atmosphere feels heavy. The administration is frequently putting out fires — moving students to different classes and new homestays, handling disputes over fees and policies.

While minor problems are sure to arise in the best of schools — and, indeed, in the best of businesses — there are ways to ensure that your school remains an upbeat, positive, fun place to be.

Prizes and gifts

Everyone loves to receive praise for a job well done; international students are no exception.

Giving prizes or gifts to deserving students — ones who demonstrate top-notch work ethic, do a stellar job on a particular project, or show tremendous citizenship during a school event — can go a long way toward building school spirit.

The prizes do not need to be elaborate or expensive, since they are gestures meant to show that students are recognized and appreciated for their effort or skills, be they academic, creative, or social in nature. A coffee mug filled with chocolates, a gift certificate for a restaurant or store, or a study aid such as a thesaurus is an appropriate gift.

Students often give gifts to teachers, staff, and homestay hosts. Since gift-giving is a normal part of the ESL world, school owners should factor the cost of gifts into their monthly expenses.

Welcome Day

Creating and maintaining a warm, friendly atmosphere should be a core goal of any school. One way to promote this is to start each term with team-building activities that allow old and new students of all levels to mix and get to know one another in a nonacademic setting.

Holding a Welcome Day at the beginning of each term is one way to promote a close-knit school. Some schools spend the first morning of a new term doing introductory activities and lessons — a school assembly in which new students are welcomed and important announcements are made, and short classes in which students are introduced to their teachers and provided with course outlines for each new class.

In the afternoon, students might take part in a range of indoor or outdoor activities (depending on the weather). Divided into teams, students could be given a task to complete. For an indoor activity, students might be asked to invent an innovative ESL-related product and create a TV commercial about it. For an outdoor activity, students might participate in mini Olympics, a treasure hunt, or a fact-finding mission.

By the end of Welcome Day, students and staff have made new and deeper bonds with each other and are excited about getting into the school routine the following day.

Sample 33 shows an example of a Welcome Day schedule and a Welcome Day Team Project.

Excursions

Like Welcome Day team-building activities, field trips and excursions have a way of uniting different groups within an ESL school. On trips away from the school, status disappears. English level is irrelevant. Students and staff become friends.

Whether it is an overnight camping trip, a weekend venture to a unique destination, or a spending spree at a famous-for-shopping city, group excursions are usually a big hit with students. However, not all students have money to spend on extracurricular outings. Also, not all students see the scholastic value of field trips, and some will view such activities as wasting study time.

There are ways to avoid creating a division between the "haves" and "have nots" in your school. One way is for the school to cover the cost of occasional outings, incorporating the cost into students' tuition fees, or writing it off as a marketing expense.

WELCOME DAY SCHEDULE

ABC Institute Welcome Day Schedule

Monday, May 2, 20--

9:00 a.m.–10:00 a.m.	Welcome to a new term! (All students and staff meet in Room A)

- Director's message
- Teacher/student introductions
- Welcome Day schedule
- Student-led facility tour

10:00 a.m.–12:00 p.m.   Orientation to classes

Mini classes (see class list for room and teacher)

10:00 a.m.–10:50 a.m.	Orientation to Academic English
	Meet teacher
	Class outline
11:00 a.m.–11:25 a.m.	Orientation to first elective
	Meet teacher
	Class outline
11:35 a.m.–12:00 p.m.	Orientation to second elective
	Meet teacher
	Class outline

12:00 p.m.–1:00 p.m.   Lunch

1:00 p.m.–4:00 p.m.   Team-building activities (All students and staff meet in Room B)

Welcome Day Team Project

Welcome Day Team Project

1. Create an ideal product or service that would enhance the life of an ESL student (e.g., a "language drink" that makes you speak English faster, or a dial-an-English-speaking-friend service).

2. Develop a one-page proposal outlining the product or service, the costs, marketing strategy, and reasons why the product or service is sure to be a success.

3. Create a short TV commercial for your product or service. You will have 90 minutes to work on your project before videotaping begins. Teams will meet back in Room A to view video clips at 3:00 p.m.

   Your team will be judged on the following:

   • Your product/service idea

   • The delivery of your TV commercial

The winning team gets prizes! Good luck!

It is always a good idea to allow students to choose whether to participate in an extra-curricular activity. Students should be encouraged to take part, but not be forced into it. To avoid problems with fees and schedules, ensure that the outings (including travel time) take place in the after-school period or on weekends. Students should not be expected to sacrifice class time, which they have paid for, for an excursion that may cost them even more money.

School clubs

Giving students an opportunity to pursue their interests and hobbies in English will set your school apart from others. By providing the space and some assistance in organizing the club, you can help students manage their own after-school activities and build their self-esteem.

Encouraging students to take the lead in their educational experiences may take some effort. One way to start is to provide students with a list of club or activity ideas based on their backgrounds. For example, a student who studied art in his or her home country might be persuaded to hold an art class once a week.

Students with more academic interests or an interest in the media might be interested in creating a student newspaper or e-zine. Students could get together once a week to discuss story ideas, writing techniques, and publication design. The work could be edited by a teacher and linked to the school's website.

Student of the term

Individual praise is a great way to build a student's sense of self-worth. It can also motivate others to evaluate their own efforts and perhaps even take their studies more seriously. One way to give individual praise is to celebrate the efforts and accomplishments of particular students on a regular basis, for example once a term.

To emphasize the importance of working hard — not to mention demonstrate the school's "customer" appreciation — the "student of the term" could be given a small gift or certificate. He or she could also be featured in the school's newspaper or e-zine.

Some schools reject the notion of promoting the skills or achievements of one student over those of another, arguing that students with low self-esteem who do not win the award may suffer from an even poorer self-image. However, with the "student of the term" subjectively chosen by staff, the award can in fact play the opposite role: it can help promote academic and social balance within the school by recognizing the efforts of those who are less gifted in the classroom.

Another way in which to ensure balance is to be aware of the gender and nationality of award winners. For example, it is best to avoid giving an honor to people of the same gender or nationality three times in a row. If a Korean male wins one term, perhaps a Japanese female could win the following term.

Parties

International students enjoy socializing with other students. However, they are eager to have the opportunity to socialize (and practice using their English skills) with native English speakers, preferably those that are about the same age as they are. Hosting get-togethers that include English speakers gives students a chance to shake their fears of communicating with "real English speakers." Equally important is that news will spread quickly that your students have unique and enviable opportunities to truly live and learn in English.

If you think starting and running an ESL school is a challenge you want to take on, read Part 4 to find out more about the practical aspects of running a business, then complete Checklist 3.

CHECKLIST 3
OPENING AN ESL SCHOOL

Before you open the doors to your ESL school, make sure you have considered the following:

- ❏ Do you have a thorough understanding of the "students as customers" concept?

- ❏ Have you researched current industry information and gained an understanding of current trends?

- ❏ Do you have a clearly defined target market that you understand well?

- ❏ Have you developed a "big picture" plan of your core programs and electives?

- ❏ Do you have a clearly defined "snapshot" of a typical term (a mapped-out system of activities from the first day to the final day of term)?

- ❏ Have you developed an evaluation system linking initial evaluation of new students to ongoing evaluations and final evaluations?

- ❏ Have you developed a student orientation system?

- ❏ Have you developed a student accommodation package?

- ❏ Have you hired a solid team of key staff and made contact with others whose services you may require?

- ❏ Have you gathered the necessary office and administration forms?

- ❏ Do you have an accessible location and adequate facilities?

- ❏ Have you created a website and marketing materials?

PART 3 EXERCISES

Exercise 17
Exploring the ESL Industry in Your Area

Make a list of things you know about the ESL industry in your region. Now consider whether there are any industry factors or trends that may have an impact — positive or negative — on your business idea.

Exercise 18
Identifying the Students for Your ESL School

Taking into consideration your industry research, employment background, and interests, briefly identify the types of students you imagine being seated in your future classroom.

Exercise 19
Identifying Programs That Suit Your Target Market

Use the checklist below to identify the programs that might suit your target market:

[   ] Academic English

[   ] English for Test Preparation (TOEFL, TOEIC, CELTA, etc.)

[   ] Grammar

[   ] Pronunciation

[   ] Practical Conversation*

[   ] Issue-based Conversation**

[   ] English for the Workplace

[   ] Job-specific English

[   ] Others not listed

---

* Practical Conversation refers to "how to" language and skills (e.g., how to ask for directions, how to explain the type of haircut you want, or how to make polite requests of your homestay host).

** Issue-based Conversation refers to language and skills used when offering your opinion and requesting clarification in a discussion, argument, or debate.

Exercise 20
Setting Your School Apart from the Competition

Brainstorm a list of things you would consider doing or offering in order to set your school apart from other schools.

Exercise 21
Exploring the Needs, Desires, and Perceptions of Your Target Market

Consider your target market. What do you know about their needs, desires, and perceptions? Can you think of anything you do not know about them but now realize you should know before pursuing them as customers?

Exercise 22
Drafting a Student Profile for Your ESL School

Drawing on your notes from Exercise 18, draft a detailed student profile for your ESL school.

Exercise 23
Drafting a Mission Statement for Your ESL School

Clarify the purpose of your programs. Draft a mission statement for your school.

Exercise 24
Drafting a Methodology Statement for Your ESL School

Draft an outline of your school's methodology for delivering on its mission statement.

Exercise 25
Drafting a Marketing Promise for Your ESL School

Create a list of things that make your school competitive and demonstrate your understanding of your market.

Exercise 26
Creating an Overview of Your School's Core Program

First, make a list of your school's core courses. Then, using the chart below, map out what a typical month might look like.

_____

_____

_____

Schedule of Core Program					
	Monday	Tuesday	Wednesday	Thursday	Friday
Week 1					
Week 2					
Week 3					
Week 4					

Exercise 27
Creating an Overview of Your School's Elective Program

First, make a list of your school's electives. Then, using the chart below, map out what a typical month might look like.

_____

_____

_____

Schedule of Elective Program					
	Monday	Tuesday	Wednesday	Thursday	Friday
Week 1					
Week 2					
Week 3					
Week 4					

Exercise 28:
Developing an Evaluation System for Your School

Outline your school's system of evaluation.

Exercise 29

Delivering Your School's Core Program

Revisit your notes on your school's core courses. Make a list of the textbooks and/or resources you will use to develop and implement each core course. Next, draft a one-month overview of the schedule for your core program.

_____

_____

_____

_____

_____

Required Textbooks and/or Resources					
	Monday	Tuesday	Wednesday	Thursday	Friday
Week 1					
Week 2					
Week 3					
Week 4					

Exercise 30
Delivering Your School's Elective Program

Revisit your notes on your school's elective courses. Make a list of the textbooks and/or resources you will use to develop and implement each elective. Use copies of the template below to draft a one-month overview outlining the materials needed to deliver each elective.

_____

_____

_____

_____

_____

Required Textbooks and/or Resources					
	Monday	Tuesday	Wednesday	Thursday	Friday
Week 1					
Week 2					
Week 3					
Week 4					

Exercise 31
Setting Up Your School's Accommodation Services

Consider which accommodation services you will offer. Make a list of the things you must do in order to set up your accommodation services.

Exercise 32
Planning Extracurricular Activities

Make a list of the extracurricular activities you would like to offer.

Exercise 33
Planning Your School's Staff

Consider the key people you plan to have working at your school. Will you or anyone else on your team be required to play multiple roles? Make a list of the roles and key responsibilities of each staff member.

Exercise 34
Planning Your School's Location and Facilities

Describe in detail your plans for your school's location and facilities.

Exercise 35
Developing a Marketing Plan

What are your key marketing strategies? Describe in detail what you plan to do in order to attract your first set of students.

Exercise 36
Developing Program and Classroom Policies

What kinds of policies and procedures do you plan to include in your new-student orientation package?

Exercise 37
Responding to Surprise Issues

What would you do to address issues such as the following two:
- Theft of electronic dictionaries, MP3 players, and other items belonging to students?
- Overflowing toilets as a result of female students attempting to flush away sanitary napkins?

Exercise 38
Maintaining and Building Your School's Customer Base

List ways to maintain and build your school's customer base.

Part 4

SETTING UP YOUR BUSINESS

Chapter 18

DEVELOPING YOUR BUSINESS PLAN

Now that you have learned the ins and outs of ESL tutoring and ESL schools, it is time to focus on the business aspects of your new venture. Even if you have years of experience teaching ESL students, if you do not know the fundamentals of setting up and running a business, it will be difficult to make a success of your operation. This section of the book leads you through everything you need to know to operate a successful ESL business. As you read through it, I encourage you to refer back to the information you read and the worksheets you completed in Parts 2 and 3 of this book, as these will form the basis of your business plan.

Every successful business needs a business plan. A business plan serves several purposes.

It provides you with a structure to follow as you work out the details of your business, from your business's name to your long-term goals to the amount of money you need to get started. A business plan can also help you access financing. Banks and other lending institutions want to see evidence that you have carefully considered your business idea. Finally, a business plan can serve as a management tool and help you keep your business on track.

Your business plan does not need to be long or complicated, and there is more than one way to format it. However, all business plans must include a number of standard sections.

This chapter provides a high-level overview of the sections you might include in an education-related business plan. For more detailed information on writing a business plan, take a look at *Preparing a Successful Business Plan*, another book published by Self-Counsel Press.

EXECUTIVE SUMMARY

The executive summary is an overview of your business plan and should therefore be written last. A page or two in length, the executive summary includes a brief summary of the following:

- Your products and services
- Your students and other customers
- You — the owner — and your key staff members (if applicable)
- Your future business goals

If you are applying for financing, you should also include in your summary the amount of money you would like to borrow, how you plan to use the money, and how the loan will benefit your business and increase profits.

DESCRIPTION OF THE INDUSTRY

This section provides general information about the ESL industry, as well as industry trends that are present nationally and in your local area, and includes the following:

- Industry facts and figures — the current number of ESL businesses in operation, how many students are studying overseas, and how much money is generated from the industry
- Industry growth potential in the short term and the long term

- Industry trends in terms of programs, location preferences, and teacher qualifications
- A brief description of how and where your business fits into the bigger picture

DESCRIPTION OF THE BUSINESS

In this section, you will want to discuss the type of ESL business you plan to open. It should include the following items:

- *Mission statement* — a brief explanation of your guiding principles
- *Programs and services* — an overview of the programs and services, accommodation services, and extracurricular services you plan to offer
- *Goals* — what and where you want your business to be in five years
- *Objectives* — concrete, measurable steps on the way to reaching your goals
- *Philosophy* — a description of what is important to you in business
- *Customers* — a brief description of your students and/or other sources of revenue
- *Business strengths* — where your business is positioned in relation to similar businesses in the ESL industry, and a description of your business's major strengths, such as highly skilled staff and experienced management
- *Type of ownership* — a legal description of your business (i.e., sole proprietorship, partnership, corporation, or limited liability corporation) and why you chose this type of ownership

PRODUCTS AND SERVICES

In this section of your business plan, you will need to provide the following details about the products and services you will offer your students and/or other clients:

- Products — program and course descriptions, activity packages

- Services — accommodation and transportation

- Fees and promotional packages, and policies regarding refunds

- Your competitive advantages and disadvantages — quality of teachers, materials, location, or tuition fees

MARKETING PLAN

A well-thought-out marketing plan is key to your business's success. In this section, you should include the following detailed information about who your students are and how you plan to reach them:

- *Market research* — refers to information and statistics gathered from secondary research (e.g., published industry profiles, studies, reports, and newspaper and online articles) and primary research (e.g., focus-group interviews and surveys of students, and information from chat rooms and weblogs)

- *Economics* — describes the size of your market, the market share you can reasonably expect to capture, your growth potential, possible barriers to achieving this growth, and how you plan to overcome these barriers

- *Customer perception of products and services* — describes the features and benefits of your programs and services, from your students' point of view

- *Customers* — details about the key student populations you want to work with (age, sex, nationality, income, needs, etc.)

- *Competition* — a detailed list of schools and related companies offering ESL programs and services, and some form of analysis that weighs your strengths and weaknesses against those of your competition

- *Niche* — a clear description of how your programs and services make your business unique, based on your analysis of competitors

- *Strategy* — a detailed plan that includes methods of capturing your target market (advertising and other forms of promotion), a promotional budget (before and after opening your business), fee information (a method of determining prices and modes of payment), your business location (in relation to your competitors), and marketing channels (brochures, agents, trade fairs)

- *Maintenance strategy* — a plan for ensuring that your students stay happy with your programs and services, and that they promote your business through word of mouth

- *Sales forecast* — a spreadsheet containing month-by-month projections of sales (registration fees, tuition fees, materials fees, etc.) for at least one year

For more information on developing a marketing plan, please see *Marketing Your Service*, another book published by Self-Counsel Press.

OPERATIONAL PLAN

Outlining the physical aspects of your business, such as its daily business hours, location, equipment, staff, policies, and licensing and legal requirements, can help ensure that you have considered all the details of its day-to-day operation. Include the following points in your operational plan:

- *Business hours* — brief description of business hours and generic schedule during a typical business day

- *Location* — details of type of building, size of work space, parking and student access (proximity to bus routes), rental and utilities fees

- *Legal issues* — business licensing requirements, industry regulations (where necessary), health and workplace safety requirements, zoning or building code regulations, insurance requirements

- *Policies* — regulations concerning student and staff conduct, refunds and extensions, program and class changes, etc.

- *Personnel* — brief description of number and type of employees and/or contract workers, qualifications and job descriptions, and pay structure

- *Equipment and inventory* — a list of everything used in your business (from furniture to computers to office supplies) along with cost estimates and supplier information

CORPORATE STRUCTURE AND SUPPORT

This section should include detailed information about the following people who manage and support your business:

- *Management and staff* — qualifications and background of you and your staff; if seeking a loan, include a résumé of each employee (see Chapters 5 and 13)

- *Professional advisers* — details and contact information for your lawyer, accountant, insurance agent, banker, and consultants (see Chapter 19)

RISK ASSESSMENT AND ACTION PLAN

This section should outline threats to your business, such as a new competitor in your area or an international crisis that reduces student travel overseas. Each threat should be followed by an explanation of what you would do to make sure your business survived the threat.

FINANCES

This section concerns money, from the amount you require to start your business to the amount of profit you expect to earn five years after starting your business.

Together, the documents listed below represent a forecast of your business's financial future:

- *Start-up costs* — detailed descriptions and prices of everything you need to get started, from equipment to legal fees

- *Twelve-month profit-and-loss projection* — a spreadsheet containing a month-by-month forecast of sales, expenses, and profits (plus a brief description of the assumptions on which you have based your major income sources and costs)

- *Five-year profit-and-loss projection (optional)* — a spreadsheet containing sales and expense forecasts five years into the future, based on things you expect to happen in the industry or in your business

- *Cash-flow projection* — a worksheet to help you forecast how much money you will need to start up and operate your business for a year without running out of funds

- *Opening-day balance sheet* — a report outlining your business's assets (items of value), liabilities (debts), and owner's equity

- *Projected balance sheet* — a report showing an estimation of your business's financial position after one year in business

- *Break-even calculation* — a calculation that determines the amount of income required for your business to be operating at a profit rather than at a loss

If you are presenting your business plan to a prospective lender, you need to show your repayment plan, including the following information:

- The amount of money you want to borrow

- How the money will be used and how this will generate revenue

- Requested terms of repayment (number of years to make full repayment)

- List of collateral

Your accountant will be able to help you prepare the financial section of your business plan, or you can take a look at *Financial Management 101: Get a Grip on Your Business Numbers*, another book published by Self-Counsel Press.

APPENDIXES

This section should include supporting documents for various sections of your business plan, such as industry studies, advertising materials, résumés, and leases and contracts.

Chapter **19**

ASSEMBLING YOUR BUSINESS TEAM

As a new business owner, you can greatly increase your chances of success by developing solid relationships with a team of key business advisers. And as your business grows in the first year, there are others in the ESL industry who are well worth getting to know.

Choosing the right adviser for your business is important. Ask friends or other small-business owners for recommendations, or look for an adviser through the Yellow Pages or local professional associations. Set up a meeting where you can get to know the person and he or she can find out more about your business. Remember that you need to be comfortable with whomever you end up hiring, and feel confident that he or she has your best

interests at heart. Do not be afraid to ask the adviser a lot of questions, particularly about his or her experience working with education-related businesses.

LAWYER

Your lawyer will assist you in making sure you have all your legal bases covered. He or she may also be able to create contracts for students, staff, homestay families, and activities organizations, such as scuba-diving companies and horseback riding associations. In the case of a dispute with a staff member, homestay host, or student (e.g., if a student threatens to sue your business for not giving him or her a refund), you will want to have a legal expert to consult. If you are planning to have students participate in off-site activities, your lawyer can help you create the necessary waiver forms.

Ideally, you would choose a lawyer who specializes in small-business matters and has a working knowledge of the ESL industry and immigration regulations.

ACCOUNTANT

Hiring a reliable, trustworthy accountant who enjoys working with small businesses is the best way for you to develop and maintain financial health. From helping you prepare your business plan to providing you with tax advice to setting up your bookkeeping system, your accountant can give you the freedom to concentrate on the aspects of your business that most require your attention — customer service, product and service development, and marketing.

For month-to-month management of income and expenses, you might decide to hire a bookkeeper. This is reasonable in many circumstances. However, there are advantages to having an accountant handle all of your financial concerns. For example, an accountant can analyze your financial information, make recommendations, and assist you if you decide you want to change your business's legal structure from a proprietorship to a limited corporation (see Chapter 20 for more information on legal structures).

When choosing an accountant for your ESL business, ideally you would hire someone who has prior experience working with education-related businesses.

BANKER

Establishing good rapport with your banker is a wise business decision. Knowing that you have access to funds when you want to expand your business — or in times of trouble — can give you the peace of mind you need to focus on building the best business possible.

Ideally, your banker would know something about the ebb and flow of the ESL industry. The best banker for you is someone whose lending and repayment requirements are in line with your business needs. If you do not already have a well-established relationship with a banker, ask your lawyer or accountant to recommend someone.

INSURANCE AGENT OR BROKER

You will also want to build a relationship with an insurance agent or broker. Regardless of the type and location of your ESL business, you will need several types of insurance, related to the building you occupy and the vehicle you use to visit or transport students. Businesses offering extracurricular activities will likely need additional types of insurance; the same applies to businesses with employees.

If you do not already have an insurance agent who knows you and your industry well, ask for referrals from colleagues until you find someone who can perform a thorough needs assessment and offer the insurance products you require.

See Chapter 22 for more information on the kinds of insurance you may need for your ESL business.

OTHER INDIVIDUALS WORTH BUILDING RELATIONSHIPS WITH

If at all possible, network your way into a friendly relationship with at least one key ESL agent in your area. (Read Chapters 7 and 15 for more information on agents.) Having an informal bond with agents, whose jobs require that they know the kinds of programs and services students are looking for (and what kinds they are *not* interested in) can help you keep abreast of industry trends. Being friendly with local agents also increases the likelihood that your business will be presented as an education option for their clients.

Other people you might want to get to know in your first year of business are people who work in the immigration field, ESL industry association members, and people who work in the accreditation field. New ESL businesses must prove themselves before being permitted to help international students gain visas to North America (see Chapter 23). ESL businesses must also have been in operation for a year or more before becoming eligible for association membership or accreditation. However, there is nothing preventing new business owners from getting to know key players in the industry and learning the ropes early on.

Chapter **20**

GETTING STARTED

What is required to get your ESL tutorial service or school started will largely depend on the type and size of business you plan to have. But whether you choose to run a home-based tutorial service or a full-service language school, you will need to ask yourself — and have answers to — a few key questions.

WHAT TYPE OF BUSINESS STRUCTURE SHOULD I CHOOSE?

Legally, there are three types of businesses: sole proprietorship, partnership, and corporation (also known as a limited liability company). Each type differs in terms of liability, taxation, and succession. In other words, there

are advantages and disadvantages to each business structure.

You should consult with your lawyer and accountant to ensure that the structure you choose matches your particular business needs. Seeking professional advice also ensures that you have the most up-to-date information about ever-changing tax laws and other key aspects of the legal system.

To prepare you for discussions with your advisers, here are highlights of the three business structures.

Sole proprietorship

A sole proprietorship is the easiest type of business to start. A sole proprietor performs all the functions of the business, accepts all profits and losses, and pays all taxes.

As a sole proprietor, you are personally responsible for all debts and obligations related to your business. This means that a creditor with a claim against your business could have a claim against your personal assets as well.

There are many advantages to a sole proprietorship, including the following:

- Low start-up costs
- Few regulations
- All decisions are made by owner
- Minimal amount of working capital is required
- Owner receives some personal-tax advantages
- Owner receives all profits

Disadvantages of this type of business include the following:

- Unlimited liability (i.e., owner is personally liable for all business debts)
- No business continuity (i.e., business dies when owner dies)
- Often difficult to raise capital
- No name protection

Partnership

A partnership is an agreement in which you and another person (or more than one person) agree to join forces to run a business. Management duties are shared, as are all profits and liabilities.

To establish the terms of a "general partnership" (such as profit-sharing details), you will need to draw up a partnership agreement. This document can protect you in the event of a disagreement or even the dissolution of the business arrangement.

In a "limited partnership," profit and loss depend on the amount of capital each partner contributes. Unlike general partners, limited partners are not involved in managing the business and may not be entitled to an equal share of the profits.

Advantages of a partnership include the following:

- Start-up costs are relatively low
- Investment capital comes from more than one source
- Possible tax advantages
- Limited regulation
- Management team is larger than in a sole proprietorship

There are a number of disadvantages, however, including the following:

- Unlimited liability (i.e., owners are personally responsible for the debts of the business)
- Authority is shared by more than one person
- Difficult to raise additional capital
- Not always easy to find solid partners
- Chance of problems arising between partners
- Each partner is legally bound by the mistakes of another partner, even if one partner acted without prior approval

- Lack of business continuity (e.g., if one partner leaves the business, it may be difficult to replace him or her with a suitable partner)
- No name protection

Corporation, or limited liability company (LLC)

A corporation is a legal entity with an existence that is independent from its members (who are also known as shareholders). A corporation can gain assets, go into debt, and even be sued, but unlike an individual, a corporation has a limitless life expectancy. Ownership interests can easily change because shares can be transferred. The corporation can continue on without any of its original members being involved.

Unlike a sole proprietorship or partnership, a corporation has limited liability. That is, no individual is personally responsible for debts or obligations that extend past the amount of share capital invested in the company.

There are many advantages to incorporating, including the following:

- Limited liability
- Some tax advantages
- Having a specialized management team
- Transferable ownership
- Existence continues beyond original members
- Separate legal entity
- Raising capital is easier

Here are some of the disadvantages:

- Must follow strict regulations regarding annual reports and other corporate records
- High start-up costs because of legal and accounting fees
- Charter restrictions dictate the number of shares an individual body (or a company) can own and put limits on the types of shares that can be voted on
- Possible double taxation of profits
- Directors can be held legally responsible in certain circumstances, such as when a director intentionally commits fraud or another business-related crime

Your lawyer or accountant should be able to provide you with advice about which business structure is right for you.

WHAT SHOULD I CALL MY BUSINESS?

Deciding what to call your ESL business can be fun. It can also be something of a challenge, since there are several factors to consider. You will need to think about students' perception of your business's name. If you are going to focus on academic learning, you will want to pick something that sounds "bookish." At the very least, you will want your name to include terms such as "institute" or "academy." If you are trying to attract the outdoor-adventure crowd, you will want a name that sounds fun or includes a term that evokes nature. However, if you are choosing a name related to the outdoors, be careful to avoid the "scary" parts of nature. For example, bears tend to conjure up terrifying images in the minds of international students.

Many English-language schools include the words "English" or "language" (or both) in their names. This may seem boring or obvious to native English speakers, especially in areas where several ESL businesses are located, but it nonetheless serves a purpose — it means that students at all levels of English ability know exactly what your business does. A school with a vague name might not attract the attention of beginner students (and these are often the students who study overseas for a long period of time).

Another important consideration is pronunciation. Think about the language limitations of your target students, and which letters and sounds they find difficult to say. For example, Spanish speakers often pronounce *y* with a *j* sound and pronounce *j* with an *h* sound, so you might want to avoid a business name that begins with *y* or *j*. Asian students typically have difficulty with *r* and *l* sounds, so you may want to avoid those, depending on your target market.

The same rule applies to spelling. You should not choose a name that is difficult, unusual, or "cute" in terms of spelling. Prospective students might be intimidated by a long, complicated name, and others might think your name is misspelled. Non-native English speakers usually do not understand clever English names, or double meanings or puns. It is better to choose a simple and solid name that gets your message across.

The best way to choose a name for your business is to first research the names of similar businesses in your area. Keep this list handy to prevent you from choosing something too similar. Next, consider the letters and sounds your students cannot easily say or spell. Keep these handy too, so that you can refer to them when making your final choice. Then think of words and images that best represent your business and what you are offering. Consider whether these are words your prospective students would easily understand and identify with. Also, think of the acronym formed by your name. Is it difficult to say? Does it spell something silly, obscene, or offensive? Once you have considered all these factors, make a list of possible names and go out and ask people — international students if possible — which one they like best, and why.

Before you begin to use your name, you'll need to make sure you have the legal right to use it by doing a business-name check at a government business-service center. You'll need this documentation in order to register your business with the government, as well as to get a business license.

The same rule applies if you are incorporating your business: you need to get legal approval from the government department responsible for business names and registrations. Companies that are incorporated must have a name that ends in one of the following terms or abbreviations: Limited (Ltd.), Incorporated (Inc.), or Corporation (Corp.).

WHERE SHOULD I WORK?

An increasing number of North American businesspeople are choosing to have home-based businesses. Home-based businesses are cheaper to operate than businesses located in commercial spaces because you do not have to spend a lot of money on overhead costs such as rent and utilities. (You can also deduct a portion of your home rent or mortgage, utilities, and other costs, including cleaning supplies if you operate a home-based business.)

There is also the convenience factor: working out of your home means no commute and therefore more time for business matters. It also means more time for family and hobbies.

While the home-based business model is certainly acceptable for a tutorial service and even a small school in some special cases, you should consider certain factors before making a final decision. First, there is the perception factor. Home-based businesses do not seem to command as much respect in the business world as businesses located in rented or leased space. More significantly, your students — paying customers who are not necessarily familiar with the home-based business model — may not take your business seriously. Or they may expect the fees to be much lower than those of a "real" tutoring business or school. If the house is large enough, has enough business features (e.g., signage, professional maintenance, a separate entrance, business furniture), and has a convenient location (i.e., close to a mall or major bus route), students may be more likely to accept the home-based school model.

Next, there are legal issues to consider. For example, you will need to find out from your municipal government if your home meets zoning requirements. Are you permitted to conduct business in a residential area, and if so, what are the restrictions in terms of hours of operation, noise, and traffic? This is especially important if you plan to use the premises for tutoring, teaching large groups of students, or meeting with business visitors such as homestay hosts, consultants, and agents. If you are only using your home office for arranging tutorial appointments by phone or e-mail, you will not have to worry about zoning bylaws.

For people who have difficulty separating their working life from their home life, a separate business location might be a mental health "must." With a commercial space, you are also likely to attract more students and staff than with a home-based business. Still, you will need to have your business inspected for compliance with health and safety regulations (e.g., whether you have enough restrooms) before your municipality will grant you a license. It is best to speak to a municipal officer about your business idea and ask for a list of criteria *before* making appointments to visit rental properties with a real estate agent. You can save time by explaining to your realtor what the commercial property must have (or have after improvements) in order for your planned type of business to flourish.

If you are relatively new to the ESL industry or have not yet established solid marketing connections that guarantee that a flock of students will arrive at your door immediately, avoid getting locked into a lease longer than one year. Getting overconfident about your business's future could backfire. What if study trends change within the year and you are locked into a building that does not match the changes you need to make? Or what if you win a large contract and do not have the space to accommodate extra students? While you could lease a second "campus," it can be difficult to find a second location that meets your needs, fits your budget, and is close enough to the original location that students feel like they are attending the same school.

Because there are different types of leases (e.g., net lease, double net lease, and triple net lease), each varying in terms of your responsibility regarding taxes, insurance, maintenance, and repair, you are advised to consult a lawyer with commercial-lease experience before signing anything.

WHAT KIND OF REGISTRATION AND LICENSING DO I NEED FOR MY BUSINESS?

Regardless of whether you work out of your home or a leased commercial space, you will need to register your business and obtain a business license. General business licenses are managed at the municipal level, so you may need to make a trip to city hall. Corporations, however, must file with a state or provincial registry. To find out where to register your business and obtain a business license, visit your local government office or contact a business service center in your area.

Criteria for obtaining a business license vary according to where you live, as well as the location and scope of your business. There are even differences between home-based businesses that receive visitors and those that do not. For example, if students, staff, and others will be visiting your home, you will have to hire an inspector to check the premises for compliance with health and safety regulations such as a proper fire alarm system, appropriate fire exits, stairways with solid banisters, adequate bathroom facilities, and outside walkways free of ruts or barriers. Parking availability may also be an issue. In some municipalities, for example, your driveway must be able to accommodate two cars other than your own in order to be given permission to receive business visitors. On the other hand, if you are using your home as an office and meeting students elsewhere, you do not need a formal inspection of the premises and you will not need to follow any parking regulations.

If you are renting or leasing a business location, you will need to obtain official zoning, health and safety, fire, and police permits before being eligible for a business license. For a comprehensive list of criteria, contact your municipal government office (or do an Internet search using the name of your city and "business license requirements").

WHAT EQUIPMENT AND SUPPLIES DO I NEED TO GET MY BUSINESS UP AND RUNNING?

The start-up equipment and supplies you need will depend on the location, size, and type of business you are starting. At one extreme, you might start a one-person home-based tutorial service in which you tutor students in their homes or in public places. At the other extreme, you might start a school in a commercial space that can accommodate 20 or more students. Or you might choose something in between. To get a sense of the similarities and differences regarding the equipment and supplies needed, consider the two extremes described below.

Home-based tutorial service office

For a home-based tutorial service office, you might be able to get by with only a well-lit, private room, but you will need to invest in a range of equipment and supplies.

Office furniture

If you do not already have office furniture — a desk and chair, lamp, filing cabinet, bookcase — you can either go to second-hand furniture stores or comparison shop at various stores that sell office furniture and supplies. Big-box stores offer competitive prices and free delivery for large items.

Office supplies

To save time and money, do one big shopping trip at an office supply store for pens, notepads, printer paper, paper clips, stapler, 3-hole punch, file folders, receipt book, large desk calendar, wipe board, and colored markers. At some stores, you can become a member and receive discounts on supplies. You can also shop online and never have to set foot in the store. This is especially helpful for tutorial services located in remote areas.

File folders can be used to store information, contracts, records, and even copies of handouts for individual students. Your receipt book will help you keep track of student payments (even if the students themselves do not need or want a receipt).

Your desk calendar and wipe board are of special significance. They can be used to organize and display an entire month at a glance. You can jot down names and appointment times on the desk calendar when receiving calls or e-mail messages. You can transfer the information to your wall wipe board (designed to look like a calendar), adding to it other business-related appointments. By using different colored pens to represent individual students and other types of appointments, you will be able to easily monitor the ebb and flow of your business. You will also be able to see, at a glance, the study trends of your market — for example, the days and times that are most popular with your students — so that you can organize your time effectively.

Business stationery

Once your business is registered, you can hire a graphic designer to help you design a logo and business image for your business cards, letterhead, envelopes, and brochures. (The same design can be used for your website, if you have one.) Some office supply stores have business-service centers that can handle the design and printing of your business stationery at a reasonable price. However, most stores do not offer services to help you write the advertising copy for your brochures. If necessary, seek help from a professional writer. Keep in mind the suggestions about promotional materials introduced in Chapters 7 and 15.

Communication equipment

Having a computer with Internet access is vital for communication, resource development, and financial management. Most international students have e-mail addresses, and many prefer to communicate initially through writing rather than having to speak over the phone. As well, many tutorial students need help with their writing. Most like the idea of sending in assignments for revisions and having them returned via e-mail. The Internet is also a wonderful resource for tutors looking for conversation topics and information, or even traditional teaching materials. As for the computer itself, all you really need is basic software — a recent edition of MS Word — and reliable Internet service. If you are doing your own bookkeeping, you may also want to buy a recent version of an accounting program.

If you do not have a computer or are in the market for a new one, shop around before you settle on one. Make sure you have a clear understanding of what is offered in terms of a warranty, technical support, and servicing/repairs. These things are important since computer trouble could have a significant impact on your business.

Along with your computer, having a printer is a must. You can use it to print business documents and teaching materials that you have created yourself or downloaded from the Internet (paying attention, of course, to copyright restrictions). Printers can also print professional-looking labels for files and envelopes. Whether you choose an inkjet printer or a more expensive laser printer, be sure to comparison shop. Do not leave the store until you have all the information you need about warranties, repairs, and replacing ink cartridges. Having to repair or replace a printer is costly, and ink cartridges are an ongoing expense.

A phone/fax machine is another useful tool, especially for business-to-business transactions and the transfer of documents (such as an application form that a student fills in by hand and needs to send in from overseas). Because it is two machines in one, you save desk space. Plus, many phone/fax machines have a photocopier function, so you can make copies of documents that are not stored on your computer. However, the photocopier function is not cost effective for large numbers of copies.

To keep your business separate from your home life, consider getting a separate business phone line, or at least a one-line system with different rings that let you know whether a caller is someone from your business life or your personal life. Phone/fax machines have useful features such as automatic redial and stored directories. One feature you *must* have is a message management service. The most convenient way to access and receive telephone messages is to order voice mail service through your telephone company, rather than having a separate message machine taking up space on your desk.

If you are a tutor on the go, a cell phone will be invaluable for fielding calls from students who are late, lost, or have to cancel because they are sick. A cell phone also gives you the freedom to run errands without missing an important call. You do not need a high-end cell phone or a plan that includes a large amount of minutes. The main purpose of your cell phone is to allow students to reach you in the event of a problem.

Teaching resources

The contents of your resource library will depend on the type of students you are working with. If you are tutoring immigrant children who are in the public school system, you will need books with exercises and activities suitable for children. If you are working with older, academically inclined students, you will most likely need a series of grammar textbooks to refer to, as well as TOEFL and/or TOEIC material. While many resources are available on the Internet, unless you have the right type of laptop and are in the right coffee shop or public place, you will not have access to these materials. Carrying books with you is one way to solve this problem. Another is to create handouts, storing them in binders in your office when you are not using them.

Contracts and other related business forms

Before you begin signing up students, you should have your filing system and forms in order. These documents are discussed in more detail in Part 2.

A school with 20 or more students

For a school with 20 or more students, your equipment and supply needs will be much the same as for a home-based office but at a much higher volume.

Furniture for the office and/or reception area

If you need office and reception area furniture — desks and chairs for office staff, chairs for guests, filing cabinets, bookcases, display tables or racks — you can try second-hand furniture stores or visit big-box stores that sell office furniture and supplies, and have competitive prices and free delivery.

Teachers' room furniture

Not all schools have a separate staff room. Instead, one classroom might be equipped with a teachers' area (tables and chairs, filing cabinets, and bookcases). Or the office might double as a resource room. A classroom might double as a staff meeting area.

If you have enough room, you can create a space for teachers to meet, take breaks, and prepare for classes. If nothing else, a few tables pushed together plus a few chairs will usually be enough. In the ideal staff room, there would be an area to sit and prepare materials, a bookshelf full of resources, a photocopier, and kitchen facilities and equipment for use during lunch breaks.

Office supplies

To get the best deals on bulk supplies of pens, notepads, printer and photocopy paper, paper clips, staplers, 3-hole punches, file folders, receipt books, calendars, wipe board and/or bulletin board, and colored markers, visit a big-box store that caters to businesses. Become a member and take advantage of discounts, online shopping, and delivery services.

Use file folders for keeping individual student records, as well as managing other aspects of program coordination (e.g., copies of course outlines, attendance lists, student surveys, teacher evaluations). File folders are also useful for organizing business forms such as application forms, homestay information, copies of financial documents, and contracts.

Receipts for tuition fees are normally provided to students registered at a school. Most often, school administrators create a receipt template they can print out and give to students upon registration. You can create this from scratch or download a template from the Internet.

Calendars, wipe boards, and bulletin boards are useful for livening up your office walls and keeping track of what is happening at your school. You can use your wipe board for reminders (e.g., a list of supplies you need to buy in a given week), staff messages, and announcements. You can also use your wipe board to map out big-picture plans or to explain to others where your business is headed. Bulletin boards can be used to post information on upcoming events, news clippings, or even envelopes for documents.

Business stationery

Your business stationery — business cards, letterhead, envelopes, brochures — helps define you and your operation, so make sure you have your logo design and stationery printing done professionally. To ensure that you get high-quality products and good service, you might want to develop a relationship with a design company that can take care of all your creative and printing needs. (With any luck, the same company will also handle websites.) You should consider getting professional help with developing content. Since the people who will be reading your materials are not native English speakers, you should be careful about the level of language you use. You might also consider finding a company that can translate your content into the languages of your key student groups.

When you are first starting out, you will likely need a large quantity of business stationery, especially brochures, because it serves two purposes — it sends a message that your business is legitimate and professional, and it gets your name out to the public and key players in the industry, such as agents.

Once your school is up and running, students will drop in looking for more information about your programs, fees, and schedules. To save money, you might want to make smaller versions of your school information and course content available to walk-in students. They will be able to take home only the information they need, instead of taking a large, expensive brochure that covers everything. That type of brochure is best suited to trade fairs and meetings with agents.

Classroom furniture

When shopping for tables and chairs, keep in mind that they will likely be moved around on a regular basis to accommodate a variety of classroom activities. While most ESL classrooms are set up with tables arranged in a U shape facing a wipe board (or in block form, where a number of tables are pushed together to form one large table), tables are rearranged frequently during small-group work and role plays. Chairs also move around a great deal, so they should be light but strong.

At least one large wipe board (with markers, erasers, and a cleaning product) should be present in each classroom. There should also be shelf or desk space for the teacher to arrange and store material.

When it comes to teaching aids, many ESL classrooms have a radio/tape/CD player, as well as a television and VCR or DVD player (for various types of listening activities), and a computer with Internet access (for looking up information and doing research projects and presentations). Having relatively new equipment is important for your school's image, so invest in up-to-date products if possible.

Furniture and equipment for student lounge and eating area

Every school needs an area where students can relax, eat their lunches, and get to know their fellow students. The furniture and equipment — sofas and end tables, a TV, tables and chairs, bookcase, fridge, microwave, coffee maker, kettle, sink, and kitchen accessories — do not need to be fancy or high end; second-hand items are fine. The purpose of the room is both social and functional, so the contents need only be clean and safe to use. By adding some pictures and plants, you can create a very comfortable space for your students to enjoy.

Communication equipment

Your office and reception area should include all the equipment necessary for communicating with prospective students, agents, homestay families, and other people and institutions you will be in contact with for regular business purposes. Computers, printers, a high-quality photocopier, a fax machine, and a business telephone are basic necessities in any competitive school.

You are also likely to need a computer area for your students. In some schools, the student lounge area doubles as a computer area. (After all, many students relax by e-mailing their friends and family back home.) The danger is that students may be careless with food or drinks around the equipment, and may damage it. If at all possible, designate a separate room as the student computer room. That way, teachers can send students into the computer room to work on assignments without disrupting people in the lounge area, and vice versa. If there is a computer in each classroom, a computer room may not be necessary. Either way, you should keep a student printer in an area that can be monitored and managed by staff to prevent misuse and to make sure the machine is operating properly.

If you need a substantial amount of equipment, you might consider leasing computers and photocopiers rather than buying them. Shop around and discuss the options available from local suppliers.

In terms of computer software, you have a number of options. Ideally, your software will allow you to create contracts and business documents, keep detailed student records, and keep track of your finances. Currently, there is software on the market that is designed specifically for managing ESL-school records and finances. One product worth considering is Language School Manager (www.language-school-manager.com). The student computers in your school should have MS Word and any other programs that might help students with their schoolwork or school activities.

Because computers and software are always changing, you might want to take your computer needs and concerns to a computer expert or supplier for some help determining which products best suit your needs.

Regarding telephone service, all you really need at the beginning is voice mail so that students and others can leave messages. You may also want to get a toll-free number once your business is up and running, which will make it easier for students to contact your school from outside your area. However, most international students will prefer to use the computer (through e-mail or a website) as a means of contacting your school from overseas.

Resources

Your school's resource collection should include a range of textbooks: a core series of textbooks that form the foundation of your programs, and a variety of specialized textbooks focusing on grammar, pronunciation, vocabulary building, writing, idioms and expressions, and other tools used for English communication (e.g., a dictionary and thesaurus). Textbooks with supplementary multimedia material such as tapes and CDs are useful as well. You are also likely to need the latest versions of books that prepare students for the TOEFL, TOEIC, and other relevant exams. Word- and language-related games such as Scrabble and Taboo are also wonderful to have on hand for times when a lighter lesson is needed to balance a particularly challenging exam or usher in the holiday season.

You should also include supplementary materials in your resource collection: stories, exercises, and assignments you and your team have created or gathered from alternative sources. A set of props for role plays is also useful. You could also include costumes (hats, wigs, and clothing), shopping-related items (empty food packages), and household objects (telephone, clock, kitchen items).

Contracts and other forms

In order to start your business off right, you will want to create all your school-related forms in advance. This includes the forms and contracts included in your student orientation package (e.g., application form, registration form), your homestay package (e.g., application form, homestay checklist), and extracurricular activities package (e.g., sign-up forms, waivers). Descriptions and samples of these forms can be found in Part 3.

You will also need to create forms and contracts related to hiring contractors and staff, if applicable. This information can be found in Chapter 23.

Chapter 21

PLANNING AND ORGANIZING YOUR FINANCES

One of the most important aspects of starting a business is financial planning and organization. The first step in looking at money matters is determining your start-up costs and ongoing monthly expenses. The second step is understanding your financing options. After that, you need to organize your financial records, keeping in mind industry-specific factors that influence the way these records are created and managed, both now and in the future.

DETERMINING YOUR START-UP COSTS

Before opening your doors for business, make a detailed list of everything you will need to have in place — and how much each item will cost. This list is an important part of your business plan and serves a dual purpose. First, it helps begin the business start-up process because it forces you to take your idea and separate it into small, practical tasks with costs attached. It can also be used later to compare against actual costs, giving you an idea of how accurate your planning and financial projections are.

Once you have spent some time with the exercises in this book, you will know what kind of business you want to start and will have a better idea of what your individual start-up costs will be. You should also consider going over your start-up list with your accountant to make sure you have included all the costs involved in starting your business.

DETERMINING YOUR ONGOING MONTHLY EXPENSES

Many of the items on your start-up expenses list will be ongoing monthly expenses. Those that come up only once or twice a year — business license fees, for example — should be included in your list, but estimated and pro-rated for each of the 12 months.

Again, once you have gone through this book and decided on the concept and location of your business, you can create a list of monthly expenses that makes sense for your business. Your accountant will be able to help you identify or clarify monthly expenses you may have overlooked.

OBTAINING FINANCING

Knowing where and how to get start-up capital is fundamental to your success in business. If your savings account is not sufficient, you will need to find money elsewhere. But before knocking on a wealthy relative's door or making an appointment with your financial institution to learn about loan options, you should prepare by understanding basic information about different types of financing and ways to access funds.

Types of financing

There are two basic types of financing. Equity financing refers to the money you have saved or are able to get through personal contacts and personal borrowing from banks and lending institutions. The main benefit of using equity financing concerns repayment: your investors share the risk and do not have to be paid back if your business fails.

The other type of financing is debt financing. This refers to money you borrow on behalf of your business, and must pay back, with interest, within a set time frame. There are several types of debt financing:

- *Short-term or operating loan*. This refers to money borrowed from a bank during peak business periods to cover the cost of extra supplies or special promotions. Typically, a fixed date in the near future (30 to 90 days) is set for repayment in full.

- *Line of credit*. A line of credit is an agreement between you and a financial institution regarding the maximum amount of credit you can use to run your business. In most cases, a line of credit is set for one year, with the possibility of renewal at the end of the term.

- *Term loans*. A term loan is money used for large purchases related to business expansion or takeover of an existing business. Term loans are repaid relatively slowly, on a monthly basis over a period of 1 to 15 years.

- *Supplier credit*. Supplier credit refers to the money you owe to a company after ordering and receiving stock and supplies. Most companies require payment within 30 to 90 days.

Where to get financing

When it comes to equity financing, a personal bank account is the most common source of capital. (In the case of a corporation, your personal funds become "shares" in the company, and you become a "shareholder.")

Another source of equity is money invested or borrowed from friends or relatives. However, such an arrangement can become problematic if the business does not perform as expected, or if the financing details are not agreed upon and spelled out in writing before the business opens. If you are planning to pursue this type of equity financing, you should first discuss documentation and taxation and interest rates with your lawyer and accountant.

As for debt financing, the most obvious option is a commercial bank. However, there are other organizations that make money available to small businesses. In the United States, the Small Business Administration assists entrepreneurs by supplementing money borrowed from a bank with a range of loan options. (For more information about loan regulations, look up the Small Business Administration in the US Government section of your phone book or on the Internet at www.sba.gov.) In Canada, the Business Development Bank of Canada performs a similar function, offering loans and other types of financing to businesses that have difficulty accessing money. (Look for the Business Development Bank of Canada in your phone book or online at www.bdc.ca.)

In many rural communities, debt financing is available from organizations devoted to economic development and small business start-up. Across the United States, USDA Rural Development offices offer business loans through banks and community-managed lending pools. (For more information, contact your local office, or find information online at www.rurdev.usda.gov.)

Community Futures Development Corporation (CFDC) is one example of a Canada-wide organization that fosters entrepreneurship and offers financing to businesses that may have difficulty obtaining loans. (To find out whether there is a CFDC office in your area, look in your phone book or online at www.communityfutures.ca.)

Whether you are seeking money from friends or relatives, a commercial bank or lending institution, a credit union, or a government body that helps new businesses get started, you will need to provide your lender with a solid, well-developed business plan. Without this, it is unlikely that lenders will take you and your business concept seriously. (See Chapter 18 for information on how to prepare a business plan.)

Other things that might dissuade a lender include the following:

- *Lack of collateral* — you need to have sufficient assets to be able to pay out your loan if your business fails

- *No financial risk or commitment on the borrower's part* — you need to show that you believe in your business idea by putting your own cash and assets on the line

- *Unclear use of borrowed funds* — your need for financing must be clearly explained, and acceptable to the lender, in order for the lender to take the risk

- *Personal issues* — if a lender lacks confidence in you because of the way you act or dress, or because you seem unstable in your personal life, they are less likely to offer financing

KEEPING FINANCIAL RECORDS

Keeping your financial records in order is vital to the success of your business. Unless you have a background in accounting or bookkeeping, the best way to ensure that your accounting system is set up properly, and that your monthly bookkeeping system is accurate, is to hire someone to do it. Not only will this give you peace of mind about your business's financial situation, it will also give you more time to concentrate on running your tutorial service or school.

The number and type of financial records you keep will depend on what kind of ESL business you choose to run. If you are operating a one-person tutorial service out of your home, your monthly record-keeping duties could involve little more than collecting in a file your invoices, bank statement, and receipts from expenditures (fuel, a portion of the rent or mortgage of your home, office supplies, etc.), and handing the file over to your bookkeeper to input the data into his or her bookkeeping system. (You could even input the data yourself using an accounting program such as Simply Accounting.) Your bookkeeper will in turn provide you with the following:

- *Comparative income statement* — a document that shows your revenue, expenses, and net income during a given month set against your year-to-date financial figures

- *Balance sheet* — a document showing your business's assets, liabilities, and equity

- *List of journal entries* — a document listing every financial transaction made during the month

If you are operating a school that has employees and offers full- and part-time language programs, accommodation services, and extracurricular activities, your accounting system and procedures will be complex and will require professional assistance. Your accountant or bookkeeper will formalize basic records into a number of "journals":

- *Sales journal* — lists daily registry of tuition fees, application fees, and other sources of income

- *Cash receipts journal* — records all types of income transactions, from cash sales to bank deposits to wire transfers from other countries

- *Accounts receivable ledger and control account* — the ledger records information about payments (date, invoice number, etc.) while the control account records all sales and payments in total

- *Accounts payable journal* — records details about invoices to be paid, helping you understand your liabilities

- *Cash disbursements journal* — records all cash outlays in a day for expenses, payroll, purchases, and loan payments

- *Payroll journal* — includes pay period, gross amount earned, and net amount earned (after income tax, employment insurance, and pension-plan deductions)

- *General ledger* — records all entries from all accounting journals combined and is used to prepare a financial statement

SETTING AND COLLECTING FEES

Before you and your accountant meet to discuss your finances and cash-flow projections, you should consider how you are going to set and collect fees from students. My best advice for a start-up ESL business is to keep it simple.

Setting fees

The fees you charge will depend on four factors:

- *Your overhead and expenses*. The lower your expenses, the more competitive your fees can be.

- *Your background and experience, as well as the qualifications of your teaching staff.* If you and your team are popular with and respected by students, you can charge more for classes and tutorial sessions.

- *Your competitors' fees.* It is best for your fees to be in line with your competitors' fees when you are starting out. (If you set your fees too low, you will give the impression that your teachers are underqualified, and if your fees are too high, you risk excluding a large group of potential students.) Once your services and programs are established and have developed a reputation, you can raise fees with less risk of driving away your students.

- *Agent fees.* If you are going to work with agents, remember that they typically ask for 20 percent to 30 percent commissions.

When setting tuition fees and organizing your bookkeeping system, you should also consider the following:

Discounts and perks. Decide whether or not to develop a reward system for students who pay several months' fees in advance. For example, you could offer sign-up incentives such as 10 percent off for fees paid three months in advance, and 25 percent off for fees paid six months in advance. You could also offer extras such as free bus passes, a weekend trip, or a small number of one-on-one tutorials. Discounts and perks would be recorded in your bookkeeping system as "promotions."

Refunds. Sometimes students change their minds about how long they want to study with you, or even how long they want to stay in North America. Sometimes they have family emergencies and must return to their home country. In these cases, students may ask for a refund. You should have a clearly worded refund policy. If you decide not to give refunds, your students must be informed of this before they sign up. If your policy uses percentages — for example, a 90-percent refund if a student withdraws within the first week of the term — you will need to include a refund entry in your bookkeeping system, or list the lost portion of tuition as a bad debt.

Collecting fees

In the case of both tutorial services and ESL schools, the simplest way to maintain financial order is to *always* collect fees in advance. Make it a strict policy that a student cannot begin attending classes before all applicable fees are paid in full (e.g., registration fee, tuition fee for the amount of time registered, materials fee, homestay application fee, homestay fee for at least one month). The same rule should apply to students who want to continue studying at the school past the last day they have paid for.

You should also request that payments be made in cash at the time of in-person registration (or re-registration). Students who do not want to carry cash could have the option of paying through direct deposit into your business's bank account. Allowing other methods of payment are unwise at the start-up stage. It is best to keep it simple, at least until your business is up and running.

It can be difficult for start-up ESL businesses to be strict about payments. What if a student has to wait a couple of days for money to be deposited by his or her parents into a bank account? Or what if the student has paid his or her agent a year's worth of tuition and pay is delayed because of the agent's incompetence? Should the student miss classes even though the money is almost certain to arrive within days of the start of a new term?

Unfortunately, even a little flexibility can be the source of numerous headaches. It is best to be consistently firm on money questions (as any established institution, such as a college or university, would be). Not only will your accountant or bookkeeper be happy, but your tutorial service or school will run more smoothly. Plus, you will avoid developing a reputation with students and agents for being "soft" or "overly negotiable." Being too accommodating can give the impression that you are not fully confident about the programs and lessons you offer.

Another factor to consider concerns your first set of students. Those attending a start-up school (or tutorial service), are not likely to come directly to you from overseas for the following reasons:

- New schools are not normally authorized to assist students with the visa permits they need to enter North America.

- Visiting students and agents often feel it is too risky to invest in a new school that has no history with students.

- It is difficult to win the trust of some students and agents when a school is not accredited or not a member of an industry association.

Since it takes new schools a year or more to become eligible for accreditation or association membership, new ESL businesses find it somewhat difficult when it comes to attracting and keeping students.

New businesses almost always have to rely on attracting students who are already in North America, students who are unhappy with where they are currently studying and are looking for alternatives. Another possible market is immigrants who need help mastering English. An advantage to this situation is that students who are already in North America are more likely to have a local bank account and understand how school fees and payment systems work. In short, since your students will most likely be familiar with the tutorial service system or ESL school, you will not have to bend your policies to win them over. Instead, you will need to be sure to offer what was missing from their previous experiences in school or with a tutor.

To summarize, your first students are likely to have the following characteristics:

- Already living in your area and looking for study alternatives

- Acquainted with you or your staff through past experiences in a school and enjoyed the lessons and service they received

- Referred by an agent you have developed a connection to

As a result, you can and should insist on collecting fees before the start of tutoring sessions or classes.

Planning for your business expenses

When determining fees and setting up your bookkeeping system, also keep in mind expenses that are somewhat unique to ESL businesses. For example, school owners who host parties and gatherings to promote a sense of community among students and staff, or between students and the homestay community, can write off party supplies as a promotional expense. Even gifts purchased as rewards for exceptional students or homestay hosts are legitimate expenses.

For a tutor who drives to and from students' homes, fuel is a significant expense. You should record your mileage for each trip. Those who tutor in public places, such as coffee shops, or go on field trips to places requiring an entrance fee, should collect receipts to give to the bookkeeper.

When you have completed the exercises in this book and have decided on the details of your business, you will be able to discuss with your accountant which purchases constitute legitimate expenses, given the nature and scope of your business.

You should take the time to consider your financial future and work with your accountant to estimate your revenue and expenses five years in the future.

GETTING CONTRACTS FOR GOVERNMENT-FUNDED LANGUAGE PROGRAMS

Across North America, newcomers to the United States and Canada are offered free English classes to help them overcome language barriers that make daily life in their new country a challenge. Organizations that provide language programs are normally well-established not-for-profit companies that offer immigrants and refugees a range of settlement services, including employment programs, translation services, and legal counseling. In some cases, however, independent operators are invited to bid on government contracts to teach language skills to newcomers.

Responding to a call for contractors — an Expression of Interest — requires a great deal of planning and paperwork. Landing a government contract is not easy — there is a great deal of competition for government-sponsored contracts (even though they often come with cumbersome regulations and monitoring procedures). However, it is possible for a new business to overcome these challenges.

Pursuing a government contract is not necessarily something you will want to do when first starting your business, since it is a time-consuming process with no guarantee of success. It may make sense to set aside such opportunities until you have a solid history of ESL-business success to include in your application. Still, it is worth keeping an eye on calls for proposals at both the state- (provincial) and national- (federal) government levels. Take note of applicant criteria, program scope and duration, and fees for services, as you may need this information when drafting your financial-forecasting documents.

If you choose the tutorial service route, you may be able to take advantage of contract opportunities sooner. Some independent contractors are hired to give English lessons as part of vocational programs. You could offer such services to immigrant organizations that do not already offer such programs.

Chapter **22**

EXPLORING YOUR INSURANCE OPTIONS

The types of insurance you need will depend on the type, size, and location of your business.

Whether you are operating a tutorial service or a school, you will need insurance for your business and, if applicable, your vehicle(s). You can buy insurance from a local insurance agency that works on contract with several insurance companies dealing with homes, cars, and businesses. Alternatively, you can work with an insurance broker who is not tied to a particular insurance company. In order to get the best service and the best rates for your business needs, be sure to compare at least three offers.

TYPES OF INSURANCE

General liability insurance covers payments for bodily injuries or damage done to others' property. It also encompasses medical, emergency, and legal fees resulting from an accident or incident. This type of insurance is a necessity for school owners operating on commercial property, as well as for home-based business owners whose students, staff, or business associates visit the property.

Automobile liability insurance covers damage to other people's property and vehicles, as well as bodily harm done to passengers in both your vehicle and other people's vehicles. As an

ESL business owner, you will likely be using a vehicle for business purposes. If you are a tutor, you will likely be driving to and from students' homes or public meeting places. If you run a school, you will likely need at least one van to take students on field trips or drive them to extracurricular activities. Be sure to purchase coverage for business use of your vehicles.

Fire and theft liability insurance is important for all types of business owners. A related type of insurance is business interruption insurance, which covers indirect losses from fire and theft, such as lost productivity and revenue.

Here are some other types of insurance to consider:

- Overhead expense insurance
- Shareholders' or partners' insurance (in the case of corporations and partnerships)
- Business loan insurance
- Life insurance
- Workers' compensation insurance

If you have employees, you might also consider group medical and dental insurance.

INDUSTRY SPECIFIC INSURANCE

Obtaining the right insurance to fit your needs requires you to know a great deal about the types of programs and services you are offering. By reading this book, you will have had a chance to start developing your business concept. You will also have the information you

need for discussions with insurance agents or brokers when looking for an insurance package that suits your business's needs.

Student health insurance

Most international students understand that it is in their best interest to have health and travel insurance when they spend time overseas. Some students purchase insurance before they leave their home country. Others purchase insurance offered by their schools. Many schools in the United States and Canada offer some form of insurance package, making things easier for students by taking care of one detail involved in having a safe and enjoyable overseas experience.

Students who buy insurance through a school must pay for it when registering and paying their school fees. Insurance costs and restrictions vary depending on the state or province. Other factors that can affect prices and types of insurance include the type of institution and the length of stay of the student. (Students attending university-based language programs often have no choice but to purchase insurance from their institution.) Some students pay as little as US$40 a month, while others pay US$70 or more for insurance.

If you are opening a school in the United States, you might want to research organizations that provide customized health and travel insurance packages. For example, International Student Insurance (ISI) has group plans for schools enrolling 5 to 50 students per month. Their standard plan covers the following:

- Medical benefits
- Emergency evacuation
- Lost luggage

- Home country coverage

- Emergency dental coverage

See www.internationalstudentinsurance .com/schools for more information, or look for other companies offering similar group insurance plans.

Similarly, some insurance companies in Canada have special services for international schools. StudentGuard Insurance, for example, offers custom-designed packages that include student orientations, staff training, an administrative helpline, and even translation services. For more information, see www.studentguard.com.

Chapter 23

HANDLING LEGAL ISSUES

We have already covered a number of things you will need to do when setting up your ESL business in order to ensure that you are operating as a valid, legal business:

- Choosing a business name

- Registering and/or incorporating your business

- Obtaining a business license (which involves a location inspection and showing proof that your business meets bylaws and zoning requirements)

- Purchasing business insurance (including insurance for vehicles, employees, and students, if applicable)

A number of other law-related issues may not be applicable to your business when you

are first starting out, but they will most certainly arise if your business continues to grow and develop. These issues are visas, industry association membership, and legal issues involved in hiring employees.

VISAS

All international visitors wishing to spend some time studying in North America need to research what form of visa will be required long before they begin their overseas travel. The process of obtaining visas can be long and laborious for students, and it can create difficulties for ESL business owners who are trying to organize classes and estimate student numbers for the upcoming term. Because the systems in both the United States and Canada are somewhat complex, especially for those unfamiliar with overseas travel, you should take some time to understand the visa application and renewal process, and your role as a business owner in the process. Bear in mind that the eligibility requirements and application processes change frequently, so keep up to date by checking government websites for the most current information.

Visas for the US

International students who want to study in the United States can apply for two types of visas:

- An F-1 (visitor) visa is for students who are primarily interested in traveling within the United States but also want to do some studying. With an F-1 visa, students can register for courses that consist of fewer than 18 hours a week of study.

- An M-1 (student) visa is for students who want to take courses that are more intensive than 18 hours of study per week or that last longer than a visitor visa allows.

Information about both types of visas can be found on the Department of State's EducationUSA website at http://education usa.state.gov/usvisa.htm.

If you run a tutorial service, you will be working with international students who have already entered the United States with an F-1 or M-1 visa. The same is true for most new ESL school owners. When you first open your business, you will most likely attract students who already have F-1 or M-1 visas but who are not satisfied with their study situation. As your business develops, however, you may begin to take in students who have come to

the United States specifically to study at your institution. When your business is at this stage, a student who applies to your school will need you to complete a Form I-20 and enter the information in the Student and Exchange Visitor Information System (SEVIS), a monitoring system created by the Department of Homeland Security. Students are required to pay a SEVIS I-901 fee for each program of study. To learn more, visit the website of the Department of Homeland Security US Immigration and Customs Enforcement at www.ice.gov/graphics/sevis/index.htm.

Students should be encouraged to apply for their visas as early as possible. Once the visas are issued, students are allowed to enter the United States no sooner than 30 days before their school's registration date.

If a student wishes to renew his or her visa in order to stay at your school for a longer period of time, you may need to generate a new Form I-20. A student visa cannot be renewed or reissued from within the United States; it must be done at an embassy or consulate abroad.

Understanding the ins and outs of the visa application process may take time, but it is in your best interest to know as much as you can about visa requirements and regulations. You can begin by visiting the website of the Department of State, Bureau of Consular Affairs, at http://travel.state.gov.

Visas for Canada

International students from some countries, including Korea and Japan, can come to Canada as visitors and study for up to six months without a special permit. Students from some other countries, including China, need a Temporary Resident Visitor Visa to enter Canada, and with this visa they can study for up to six months. In both cases, however, a student who wishes to continue studying longer than six-months must leave the country in order to apply for a Study Permit. For this and other reasons, it is recommended that overseas students apply for a Study Permit if they intend to study in Canada. With a Study Permit, a student can stay in Canada for the duration of his or her program, even if the program lasts several years.

Having a Study Permit means students can do the following:

- Work part time on the campus of their college or university (if registered as a full-time student)

- Apply for renewal of their Study Permit from within Canada (without having to leave the country)

When overseas students apply directly to your school, you will need to write them a Letter of Acceptance so that they can proceed with the visa application process. The letter must include information about the type and length of the program the student has been accepted into. Students should apply for a Study Permit as soon as they receive your Letter of Acceptance. Processing times vary at different visa offices.

If you run a tutorial service, you will be working with international students who have already entered Canada with a Study Permit or Visitor Visa (or simply a passport in the case of a short-term stay), or immigrants who need help improving their English. Therefore it is unlikely that you would be dealing directly with visa issues, but it would be helpful to understand the process in case your students have questions.

As an ESL school owner, having a solid understanding of the Canadian visa application process is in your best interest. To learn more about the system, including what is required in a Letter of Acceptance, visit the Citizenship and Immigration Canada website at www.cic.gc.ca/english/study/index.html.

ACCREDITATION AGENCIES AND INDUSTRY ASSOCIATIONS

Accreditation agencies and industry associations serve several purposes. Most importantly, they protect international students who have traveled a long way and have spent a great deal of money in order to improve their English, academic, and/or vocational abilities. Without this type of protection, international students can be vulnerable to fly-by-night ESL schools, which have been known to disappear with students' tuition fees. Students can also be vulnerable to poorly managed institutions with underdeveloped programs and under-qualified teachers. Either way, it is bad news for the ESL industry when students have bad educational experiences.

Neither accreditation nor membership in an industry association is mandatory, but they do make it easier for a school to help students enter the country. In the United States, this means being able to generate a Form I-20 for a student who has applied to your school from his or her home country; in Canada, it means being recognized as legitimate enough to issue a Letter of Acceptance that is recognized by the Citizenship and Immigration department.

While there are tremendous benefits to getting a formal stamp of approval from the government and an industry association, both require that a school be in business for a year or more (and conform to a number of regulations concerning finances and teacher qualifications) before applying. What this means is that new businesses must be creative and vigilant in finding "customers" and staying open long enough to become eligible for the bigger and better marketing opportunities that come with accreditation. Still, many smaller operations manage to attract enough students — even if they are only short-term students with visitor permits — to run a successful business, with or without having accredited programs or membership in an industry association.

If you want your business to eventually gain accreditation and membership in an industry association, you should familiarize yourself with the requirements. Business owners in the United States can begin by visiting the following websites:

- Commission on English Language Program Accreditation (CEA) www.cea-accredit.org

- Accrediting Council for Continuing Education & Training (ACCET) www.accet.org

- American Association of Intensive English Programs (AAIEP) www.aaiep.org

Business owners in Canada can visit the following websites:

- Canadian Association of Private Language Schools (CAPLS) www.capls.com

- Canadian Language Council (CLC) www.c-l-c.ca

- Private Career Training Institutions Agency (PCTIA) www.pctia.bc.ca

HIRING EMPLOYEES

When you first start your business, you may not need to hire employees; you may get by working on your own, with your business partners, or by hiring instructors on contract. However, once your school or tutorial service starts to grow, you will likely require employees.

Before officially hiring anyone, you will need to do the following:

- In the US, obtain an employer identification number, also known as a Federal Tax Identification Number, assigned by the Internal Revenue Service

- In Canada, apply for a business number, issued by the Canada Revenue Agency

- Register with your state or provincial department of labor

- Set up a payroll system (with the appropriate mandatory deductions)

- Obtain workers' compensation insurance

- Display employment standards notices at your business

For details on regulations for hiring employees, contact your state Department of Labor (in the US) or your provincial Ministry of Labour (in Canada). You can also find information on the following websites:

United States

- Internal Revenue Service www.irs.org

Canada

- Canada Revenue Agency www.cra-arc.gc.ca

- Government of Canada —
  Business Start-Up Assistant
  www.bsa.cbsc.org

Though not required by law, you will want to set up personnel files and create an employee handbook containing regulations specific to your business.

Teachers and staff at ESL businesses are not normally required to undergo a criminal record check, nor are there any laws regarding qualifications or teaching licenses in the private ESL industry. (Though, as discussed earlier, your staff's formal credentials are considered when you apply for accreditation or association membership.) This does not mean, however, that you should not set employee standards for your business. For information on the number and types of employees you might want to hire, see Chapters 5 and 13. For more information on human resources practices, see *Employee Management for Small Business*, another book published by Self-Counsel Press.

PART 4 EXERCISES

Exercise 39
Choosing a Name for Your Business

1. Names of similar businesses in my area:

   _____

   _____

   _____

   _____

2. Letters and sounds ESL students cannot easily say:

   _____

   _____

   _____

   _____

3. Images and words that best represent what my business is:

   _____

   _____

   _____

   _____

4. Short list of names:

   _____

   _____

   _____

   _____

Consider the following:
- Will my students be able to easily say and spell these names?
- What acronym does each name form?

Don't forget to —
- test the names with friends and potential students, and
- check with the government department that handles business registration in your area to find out whether the names are already being used.

5. The name of my business is:_____.

Exercise 40

Determining Your Start-up Costs

Item	Start-up cost ($)
Accounting and legal	
Advertising and promotion	
Bank account start-up fees	
Business registration, licenses, and association fees	
Business-related vehicle costs (insurance, special license, fuel, maintenance)	
Consulting and research	
Equipment and furniture	
Insurance	
Office supplies	
Program-development fees (if using outside help)	
Rental deposit and first month's rent (if not a home-based operation)	
Repairs and improvements	
Teaching supplies and resources	
Telephone hookup and first month of service	
Internet hookup and first month of service	
Utilities hookup and first month of service (if not a home-based operation)	
Other expenses:	
Total	$

Exercise 41

Determining Your Ongoing Monthly Expenses

Item	Monthly expense ($)
Accounting and legal	
Advertising and promotion	
Bad debt	
Bank fees	
Business association fees	
Business-related vehicle	
Consulting and research	
Contractor's fees and/or employee wages and benefits	
Equipment and furniture	
Insurance	
Internet	
Office supplies	
Rent	
Repairs and improvements	
Teaching supplies and resources	
Telephone	
Utilities	
Other expenses:	
Total	$

OTHER TITLES OF INTEREST FROM SELF-COUNSEL PRESS

FINANCIAL MANAGEMENT 101:
GET A GRIP ON YOUR BUSINESS NUMBERS

Angie Mohr, CA, CMA
ISBN 10: 1-55180-448-4
ISBN 13: 978-1-55180-448-4
US$14.95 / CDN$19.95

Financial Management 101 is the second book in the *Numbers 101* series. This book covers business planning, from understanding financial statements to budgeting for advertising. Angie Mohr's easy-to-understand approach to small-business planning and management ensures that the money coming in is always greater than the money going out!

"Even Microsoft and Ford started in someone's basement or garage," says Angie Mohr. "But people all over the world have been given an idealized and unrealistic view of how to operate a business, and most discount the importance of the basics."

Financial Management 101 is an in-depth but easy-to-read guide on business planning. It's a kick-start course for new entrepreneurs and a wake-up call for struggling small-business owners.

MARKETING YOUR SERVICE

Jean Withers and Carol Vipperman
ISBN 10: 1-55180-395-X
ISBN 13: 978-1-55180-395-1
US$18.95 / CDN$24.95

To effectively sell your service business, you must let people know that you exist *and* that you are better than your competition — in other words, you need to market. However, owners of service businesses are often inexperienced in marketing and unsure how to promote themselves in a professional manner.

This book explains how to develop a marketing plan that will work for any service business — from law firms and dental practices to hair salons and auto repair shops. Whatever your business, it will profit from expanding your market.

The authors, who are both consultants to service businesses, have provided more than 30 worksheets to help you develop your own specific marketing plan based on the program they describe. The book answers the following questions and more:

- How does marketing a service differ from marketing a product?

- How do you prepare for marketing?

- Where can you find information about potential clients?

- Can you effectively use the Internet to market your services?

- What should you know about your competition?

- How do you establish desirable and realistic goals?

- What strategies for pricing and promotion will work best for you?

- How do you develop and implement an action plan for marketing?

This edition comes with numerous worksheets to get you started and keep you organized, all included on a CD-ROM.